ALL THE KINGS' HORSES

MARY KING AND
ANNIE COLLINGS

ALL THE KINGS' HORSES

DAVID & CHARLES

Page 1: William in his element, galloping freely on he steeplechase at Badminton n 1996
Page 3: Boris' pre-Badminton run at Belton in 1989
Right: Mary and William through the water at he 1996 Olympics in Atlanta

PHOTOGRAPHS by Iain Burns unless otherwise acknowledged. The author and publishers would like to thank the following for supplying additional pictures for his book: Mary and Annie pp10(btm), 11(top/btm), 12, 6(top/btm), 17, 20, 21, 22, 3(all), 26–7, 29, 34–5, 45, 6(btm), 66, 67, 70, 84, 87(all), 8, 98, 101, 108, 109; Srdja Djukanovic p95; Equestrian Services Thorney pp38–9, 02(top/mid); Kit Houghton pp2, , 4–5, 9, 10(mid), 16(mid), 8–19, 25, 32, 47, 52–3, 54–5, 59, 2, 65(top), 74, 75, 82, 90–1, 94, 02(btm), 106, 114, 128; Bob angrish p71(top); Nick Morris 65 (btm)

A DAVID & CHARLES BOOK

WRITTEN BY DEBBY SLY

First published in the UK in 1997

catalogue record for this book s available from the British brary.

SBN 0 7153 0543 3

rinted in France by mprimerie Pollina S.A. or David & Charles runel House ewton Abbot Devon

CONTENTS

Behind every successful eventing partnership there has to be a hard-working and dedicated team of people who are prepared to devote themselves selflessly to the ambitions of both horse and rider. Mary King is no exception: throughout her career she has received help and support from her parents, who were happy to encourage her in her love of riding from an early age; from David King, now her husband, who helped Mary buy King Boris, so setting her on the road to fame; and from her sponsors: originally the Carphone Group, and now Gill Robinson, a former director of the group, and Frizzell Countryside Insurance, who supported Mary and her team from 1995–6.

Mary's story is one to inspire every horse-mad teenager. Her parents had no previous connection with horses; with some initial reluctance Jill Thomson found herself leading her small yet determined daughter around the Devon country lanes on the vicar's pony, Magpie, little realising what the future held in store. Riding borrowed ponies, Mary became an active member of the Axe Vale Pony Club, with whom she first visited Badminton at the age of 11, and developed a burning ambition to compete there. On leaving school she worked for three-times Badminton champion Sheila Willcox for two-and-a-half years, and is eternally grateful to Sheila for the tremendous amount of knowledge and experience instilled in her during that time. She set up on her own in 1979, teaching riding from a rented disused farmyard on the outskirts of Salcombe Regis, and doing all kinds of odd jobs to enable her to compete and to start her on the road to her international eventing career with her fantastic string of 'King' horses.

But there is another unobtrusive and yet vital member of Mary's back-up: Annie Collings, her head girl from 1985 to the end of the 1996 season, who provided Mary with the most direct support on a day-to-day basis. Annie had previously worked for the Master of the local hunt, Martin Salter, and his wife Phil.

Left: Annie gets on with plaiting William, while Mary discusses tactics
Above: Mary signs autographs for some of her many fans

Tina Court, one of Annie's best friends, was partly responsible for Annie joining Mary's team. Also a local Devon girl, Tina had heard about Mary through the local Pony Club. After she left school she studied at Bicton Agricultural College, then went to work as a groom at the local riding school. She first met Mary at a Young Farmers' event, where Mary was giving a dressage and showjumping demonstration. Tina explains how she made her first approach to Mary, at a local event:

'I went up to her afterwards and asked her if she wanted any help in her yard. She was charming and polite, but explained that until she could gain some sponsorship she couldn't afford any help. However, just a few months later her sponsorship deal with the Carphone Group was confirmed and, true to her word, she telephoned me and asked if I still wanted a job. I leapt at the chance and soon settled into the routine. At this time Mary had only a few horses: Diver's Rock, Boris (who was just a baby then), King Max, and Crown Gold, a stallion that Mary had on loan. The day I arrived also saw the arrival of Silverstone, a horse belonging to the Pinders, who later bought Star Appeal for Mary. She had the yard extremely well organised, and yet still managed to keep a happy, relaxed atmosphere.

'I had only been there a few days when I was left on my own for the first time as Mary was going to an event. Soon after she left, the local farmer arrived with a delivery of straw that he said Mary had told him to stack in one of the stables. Once he finished I noticed that the stallion, Crown Gold, could reach the straw stack from his stable and was happily munching away. I knew from my stable management books that horses weren't meant to eat straw as it could give them colic, and I didn't know *what* to do! It's all very well knowing these things in theory, but in practice I didn't know how much they could eat, or how quickly they might become ill. So I tied him up so that he couldn't reach it and then rang Mary who, thanks to her sponsorship, obviously had a car phone! Apparently Crown Gold always munched a little bit of straw from his bed, so she thought a little extra from the stable next door wouldn't do him any harm.

'By the time I had worked there for about six months, Mary decided we needed more help because the number of horses she had was growing, and she now needed someone who could travel to events with her to help as well as someone to stay in the yard and look after those left behind. I had known Annie since we were both very young and knew that she would love the job. She had been away at Porlock and I had been at Bicton, so we hadn't really seen much of each other for a few years – and in those first few weeks I don't think Mary had full value for money out of us because we had so much news to catch up! The yard still wasn't that big, and with the two of us it was quite easy to get everything done in good time; so we would then go off to the beach for an hour and a half at lunchtime, or down to the pub. When Mary came up in the afternoons she would send us off to rake the sand arena and we would get so exhausted chatting to each other and recovering from our lunch-break that we would just *have* to sit down and sunbathe for a while! We got very good at recognising the sound of her jeep coming up the lane, and would leap up and rush to the opposite ends of the school and start raking frantically! It's funny to look back at how easy and relaxed it was then, compared to how busy it is now. And Annie is so dedicated in spite of the long hours she has to work.

'Once my son was born, I worked part-time for Mary until she had the full time help she needed. Even now I still go in and feed the horses if they are short staffed and away at an event. I work full time at the Donkey Sanctuary now, organising the transport, so I still see plenty of Annie, either during the week or when she comes to us to work for the few winter months when there is nothing to do in Mary's yard.

Above: Angela Pinder's horse Silverstone, a horse which helped Mary at the start of her career

Left: Cricket the mouser gets his reward

'Looking back, it was a brilliant period for both of us – we were just a couple of young girls fresh out of college, and Mary took us on and gave us the chance to ride some fantastic horses and go to some wonderful events.'

At this point, Annie takes up the story, 'When I left school my parents didn't really want me to work with horses because the wages are usually so low, but I think they realised quite quickly that they weren't going to be able to put me off! As a small concession I did stay on at sixth form, but I can't say it did me much good. As far as being prepared for life as a groom, my sister was a great influence as she always made me do everything properly, even when we just had a pony to share between us. I trained at the Porlock Vale Equitation Centre, which I had first visited years earlier with the Pony Club. I remember thinking then that it was *the* place to be! It gave me a brilliant grounding, and it's probably just as well that they were so strict; it was very good discipline, although it always seemed a pain at the time. I will never forget the blue headscarves we had to wear, and how they went wild if you wore make-up! I studied for my AI while at Porlock, but couldn't actu-

Below: David Green 'rescues' Mary at a celebrity challenge at Bramham, in 1987; and Annie on Dobbin

ally take the teaching exams because I did not have English 'O' level, which was one of the requirements then.

'When I finished I really wanted to get a job near home. Dad had heard that Martin and Phil Salter were looking for a groom; I think I got home from Porlock one day, saw Martin that night, and started work next day! I really loved my two years there; they treated me like one of the family, taking me to the races and letting me have plenty of days' hunting.'

There were about fifteen hunters and point-to-pointers in the Salters' yard, and Annie hardly knew how to fill her time when she moved to Mary's yard and found only four or five cosseted event horses to look after!

Mary recalls, 'Poor Annie was used to having to do everything in such a rush that when she first came here she put everything into a complete spin! A friend of hers, Tina, was already working for me, and in time they complemented each other well. Tina was extremely conscientious, and a steady, methodical worker – Annie would storm around doing everything in half the time, but probably only half as well as Tina! So Tina taught her to take a little more time to get things done properly, while Annie encouraged Tina to speed up a bit...and it worked!'

Annie laughs as she remembers looking round the yard and trying to work out why Mary wanted her help as well: 'but I soon realised that the event horses needed much more time spent on schooling each day than the hunters or point-to-pointers. And

Centre left: Mary's mother, Jill, takes a welcome break at Burnham Beeches
Left: The end of many a hectic season meant holidays in exotic places for Mary and Annie

Below: Eventing often means being on call late at night: Annie still on duty at midnight, at Bramham

the rest of the time was soon filled with grooming, clipping and trimming, tack cleaning and generally keeping the yard and lorry spick and span. My first attempt at clipping one of Mary's horses was pretty disastrous, though – it was only my second day at the yard and I had to clip Silverstone, a grey horse. Halfway through the clipper blades went blunt, so I found another set and carried on. It was only when I'd finished and looked at both sides of the horse that I realised that the second set of blades were 'fine cut', which meant that one side was clipped tight to the skin and looked really dark, while the other side was much lighter and hairier. I don't think Mary was too impressed with the two-tone effect! It taught me a lesson, though, and now I'm really fussy about how they finally look, and always make sure I have plenty of time to do the job properly.'

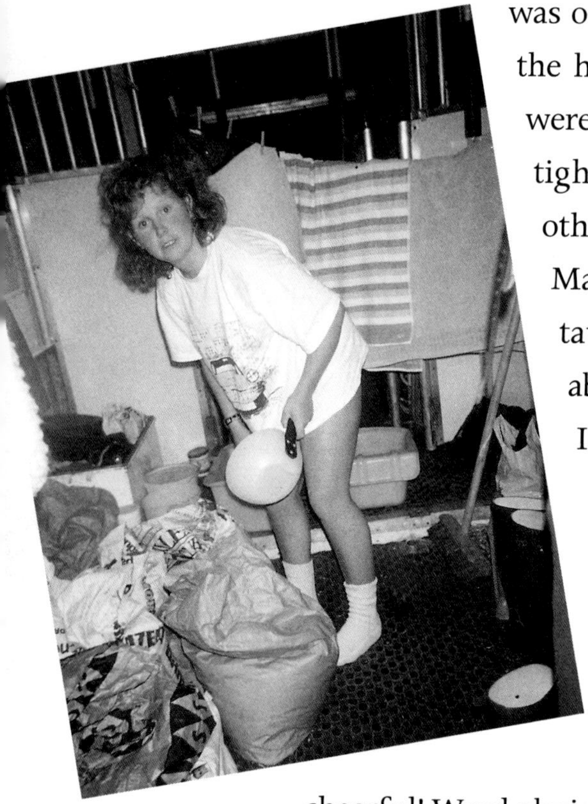

A lucky coincidence led to Annie getting a job with Mary. Mary used to see Annie driving past the yard in her Mini each day, and 'I was giving her elder sister riding lessons at the time, and I think I must have mentioned that it would be really nice to work with someone who looked so cheerful! Word obviously got back to Annie, who came for an interview and so joined the team.' 'Leaving the Salters' yard was quite a wrench,' says Annie, 'but making that decision has meant that I've been able to travel all over the world and work with some brilliant horses.'

Annie was born in Sidmouth in 1966, the youngest of four daughters.

'I went to our local riding school when I was about five, mainly because all my sisters had lessons there and I didn't want to be left out. I was quite frightened of the ponies and certainly didn't want to ride them to begin with. I used to stick next to the lady who ran the school, Daphne Banks, but gradually I found sufficient confidence to have a go at riding. The first pony I ever sat on was called Dobbin, and he wouldn't go faster than a walk, which suited me just fine! But it wasn't long before I wanted to do more, and I took part in all the Axe Vale Pony

Club activities. Dad bought two ponies for us to share, and we did a bit of everything with them.'

Annie already knew of the adventures of Mary Thomson; Mary had been a member of the Axe Vale, and was already something of a legend in the local equestrian community.

'I do remember thinking she must be brilliant because she had passed her Pony Club H test which, in my eyes, meant she must know just about everything there is to know about horses. I knew that she had moved away to work for Sheila Willcox, but was most disappointed to find myself competing against her in the show ring one summer – she must have had a rare weekend off – when we were both in the best rider class; she won it and I came second. All I could think was that if only she could have stayed at Sheila's that particular weekend I would actually have won a trophy!

'Moving to Mary's yard was easier than I thought it might be. It was helped by the fact that I already knew Tina, but even if I hadn't there wouldn't have been a problem; Mary creates such a good atmosphere in the yard, and the horses are so fantastic, that I'm sure I would have settled in very quickly anyway. Because the yard is in a small village, and Mary is so well known, the job is very sociable because everyone you meet around the lanes knows you, and wants to hear how Mary is getting on. Hacking out can take a lot longer than you intended!'

Mary has always worked hard to ensure that she has a good working relationship with her staff.

Right: 'And then he *threw* his head up and broke into canter...' Mary is renowned for her extravagantly expressed accounts of the horses' performances

M920 AWS

Left: All in a day's work for Annie: roadwork on Apple. Devon provides a lot of good long hills, excellent for getting the horses fit

'Having seen how hard grooms at other yards had to work, and how little credit they were given, I was determined that whoever I employed would be treated like a friend and would be made to feel they were an essential part of the team.'

Annie's enthusiasm and loyalty indicate that Mary has certainly succeeded in her aim, and while Mary's competition success has meant that Annie has attended the world's most prestigious equestrian events – the Barcelona and Atlanta Olympic Games, two European and two World Championships, as well as all the major three-day events in Britain and Europe – she still feels that the most rewarding part of her job is seeing the young horses gradually mature and develop their own characters, which helps equip them for life at the top of their sport. She loves having the chance to watch the horses compete, but she also likes seeing how they cope when Mary goes on team training courses, or for lessons with Ferdi Eilberg.

There are, of course, some slightly less attractive aspects of the job: Annie concedes that it's quite hard to see friends planning to go off for the weekend when she knows she has to work. The early starts are quite difficult, too, especially for a keen partygoer like Annie – 'but I actually find mucking out quite relaxing! Especially if I've had a good night out and am still suffering the consequences...' – and muddy horses on a cold winter's day are a definite pet hate! But the good outweighs the bad: Annie has made some good friends on the eventing circuit, and has had the opportunity to travel abroad.

Right: A day's tuition with Mary is always a popular competition prize. Here she demonstrates the position of the leg during jumping

Below: Mary and Annie did four years with Riders for Romania – this is the 1993 team
Centre: Mary with Gill Robinson who has given her great support over the years

'The great thing about being an eventing groom is that everyone in the sport is so friendly – I always have someone to run to if anything goes wrong, or if I've forgotten anything. Someone, somewhere, is willing to help. The Dutch rider, Eddie Stibbe, always has a very well

equipped lorry, so I usually go there first! I have never yet forgotten to load up the horse, though I do believe that Ginny Elliot arrived at an event once, let down the ramp and found that the horse was still at home. But Mary nearly turned up at one event without me when, after we stopped to fill up with diesel, I went off to the loo and came out to find the lorry disappearing off down the road without me!'

She is also fortunate in that she works in a yard where all the horses have the opportunity to fulfil their potential. Many event riders have to run large strings of horses for many different owners in order to make a living, but Mary has never been under quite the same pressure; she has never had more than

seven horses in the yard, and they are all owned either by Gill Robinson, or by David and Mary. Each horse is given the necessary time to learn his job properly and, for a dedicated groom like Annie, that makes the whole job even more worthwhile; and an added bonus has to be the fact that she could keep her beloved King Cuthbert in the yard too. Bertie, with King Boris, was one of the original members of Mary's team of Kings.

Above: Mary and William Fox-Pitt on a photo shoot for the *Tatler's* Veuve Cliquot sporting calendar

EARLY HORSES

After Mary finished her two years of training with Sheila Willcox she took a year out from horses to do a Cordon Bleu cookery course and to work as a chalet girl. However, she returned home to Salcombe Regis still determined that horses were to be her career, and to make her mark as an event rider.

'My plan was to buy one reasonably experienced horse on which to start competing and then to bring on one or two youngsters which I would produce to sell, in the hope of making sufficient profit to finance my competing. I didn't have that much money to spend so I knew it would be difficult to afford a horse which was very experienced, but **HUMPHREY**, who was advertised in *Horse and Hound*, sounded as if he might be suitable. He still only had novice points, but he had gone clear round some intermediate tracks. I remember walking into the yard where he was and seeing this really cheeky face leaning out of its stable watching me. He was a 16.2hh English Thoroughbred with enormous character, and I fell for him straightaway. He was seven or eight when I saw him, and he belonged to Col Tadzik Kopanski who is in charge of the Pony Club; and it was through buying Humphrey and keeping in touch with the Kopanskis that I met Graham and Gill Thomas who became my sponsors.

'Things did not get off to a smooth start when Humphrey failed the vet because he made a noise in his wind when he galloped; but I knew I was unlikely ever to find anything else with as much experience for such a reasonable price, so decided to have him anyway.

'I rode him at only a few novice events that summer before trying our first intermediates together – and he won three in a row! His dressage wasn't particularly good because he would become highly excited, and we both struggled a bit in the showjumping phase – but he made up for it all across country. He was very fast, and at the time I was riding far too fast across country; I was very ambitious to succeed, and seemed to have no fear at all – we must have been quite frightening to watch! Nevertheless I felt confident enough to try an advanced class that autumn: Humphrey produced a reasonable test, for him, and I then remember going absolutely flat out across country, naively assuming that as this was advanced level the only real difference was that we would have to go faster – and we won it! I just thought "Wow, this is all so easy!" I really thought I had cracked it and was about to hit the top. We went to Osberton at the end of our first season: it was my first three-day event, and we were beaten into second place by Mark Todd. So then I was utterly convinced that I had made it!

'We came out the following year feeling immensely confident, only to discover very quickly that we were paying the price for going too fast across country. I had two bad falls in quick succession, both at upright fences where I simply came in much too fast and on too long a stride.

'After the first one I suffered only concussion, but the second fall at Hagley Hall, left me with concussion, broken ribs, and my ear almost torn off – it was just starting to dawn on me that there was more to eventing than going fast. I started to watch what the top riders did, began to appreciate some of the finer points of balance and rhythm and attempted to put it all into practice. We managed to stay on our feet at the next few events, and as a result were long-listed for the Young Rider team and asked to compete in the final trial at Bramham three-day event. I was now 21, and it was only my second season in eventing, but it was the last year in which I would be eligible for Young Rider teams [for riders aged 18-21].

It was a week of soaring temperatures and we were all being warned *not* to push our horses too hard on the cross-country. It was all quite an eye-opener for me, because there *were* horses finishing extremely tired and having to be put on drips to get fluids into them quickly. So I did go slowly, but clear across country; but Humphrey had pulled a shoe off and was too sore to showjump on the final day.

'I rode him at only a few more advanced events before he strained a front tendon. He had a whole year off, but sadly, each time he came back into work it would flare up again, and each time it was getting worse. Finally I was advised by the vet to have him put down. It was a horrible experience; he had been my first competition horse, he had given me a fantastic first season, and then it all came to an end. This was the start of a really bad time for me; over the next year I lost another horse, King Rollo, found to have navicular, and then Diver's Rock, who gave me my first ride round Badminton, was also diagnosed with navicular and also had to be put down in the end. Fortunately I had made the big decision, right in the beginning, to insure the team of three horses that I kept in the yard. Insurance is always a big expense, and when you have no backing and are struggling to get started it is the sort of thing you might cut back on; but if they had not been insured it would probably have broken me completely and I would never have been able to have kept going.

'Humphrey's career was short-lived but he did me the greatest possible favour as it was thanks to him that I met my future sponsors. I had kept in touch with the Kopanskis, Humphrey's previous owners, and they could see that I was ambitious and also very keen to succeed. A relative of theirs worked for the Carphone Group and knew that the directors of the company, Gill and Graham Thomas, were keen to become involved in eventing. So the Kopanskis organised a dinner party which brought us all together, and which resulted in the very generous sponsorship which has continued throughout my entire career, thanks to Gill Robinson's [formerly Thomas] unending support and friendship.'

Above: Mary and Humphrey flying along and going too fast – as was usual!

Mary bought **ARTHUR** *shortly after she had acquired King Max, and came across him through her friends the Kopanskis, from whom she had had her first competition horse, Humphrey. And the close connections didn't end there, because Arthur actually belonged to Clare Rushworth who was later to sell King Kong to Mary.*

'Arthur was a lovely, substantial Irish Thoroughbred. When I tried him his jump was not that good, but he did move very well, with a big round stride. He was well put together with a huge powerful bottom and shoulders, narrowing down to quite a thin neck, but it did give him a wonderful galloping stride. At that stage I used to choose a horse mainly on their conformation and movement, and never worried too much about their jump, always feeling that I could improve that. Experience has since taught me, however, that a good jump is almost the number one priority! It is far easier to improve a horse on the flat than it is over fences. And Arthur remained, throughout his career, quite a careless showjumper. He was a very relaxed horse, so that could not be used as an excuse for his carelessness – he just didn't seem to mind hitting fences. Whereas William, for example, tries very hard *not* to hit the fence, but his technique and athleticism are invariably compromised by the tension and nerves he suffers at three-day events.

'In spite of this, Arthur was extremely successful at novice and intermediate one-day events. And as a seven-year-old, in what was his first full season eventing, he went to Osberton with Max and won his section! The following year he won the Windsor three-day event and, unlike Max, I really did feel he had the scope to go on to greater things. He went to Boekelo that autumn where he was superb across country, but then had *five* showjumps down on the last day; this was bad even for Arthur, and left me feeling very disheartened. However, I worked hard on his jumping all winter and was looking forward to great results in the spring. But whilst out hacking with one of my working pupils, Arthur spooked at something in the hedge and whipped round in the road – it was just a silly, freak incident but it resulted in a tendon injury to his hind leg. He had six weeks rest, followed by controlled exercise in hand; then he was sedated so that he could be turned out in the field to give the tendon more time to strengthen up naturally. But within three months it had come up again. In spite of more rest, every time we tried to work him again the injury blew up again and it was worse each time.

'Eventually the decision was made to have him put down. I missed him a great deal; he had always been a very kind horse and a real gentleman. We all called him Uncle Arthur, because even as a youngster he seemed to be older than his years. Although injuries to hind tendons are relatively rare, Arthur had always had what they call a "shivering hind leg": if you moved him backwards, his leg would shiver and shake. No one could find any reason for it, and it never affected his soundness, but perhaps it just indicated a weakness which came to a head with his second injury.'

Left: Early success for Arthur when he won at Osberton in 1986 – his first three-day event
Above: He also won his second three-day event, at Windsor the following year

KING MAX *was one of the first horses Mary bought after being offered sponsorship by the Carphone Group. She was at Badminton where she was preparing for her first ride on Diver's Rock in 1985; and at the traditional cocktail party Graham and Gill said they would like to buy her two young horses to bring on and compete.*

'I wasted very little time starting to look! I came across Max by accident, really. His owner lived in the next village and was going on holiday so I had him at livery for a couple of weeks. It had never really occurred to me that he might be the sort of horse to buy to event – but he grew on me! He was six years old when he came, and although he was small he had lovely big, loose natural paces. He wasn't particularly well schooled, nor was he in brilliant condition, but he had very good conformation and I did like his character very much. That first year I just played around with him, taking him to local shows and hunter trials, and brought him out "properly" the following season as a seven-year-old. Max took to eventing very well – his showjumping was his weakest point, but as with many of my earlier horses, I know it was my weak spot as well, so the problem was probably 50:50! He upgraded to intermediate in his first season and we went to Osberton as our first three-day event together. He was leading up until the last day, but then we had a stop in the showjumping which took me very much by surprise, and which dropped us to fourth. I had King Arthur there at the same time and he won his section.

'By his second season he was nearly advanced, and while he had coped extremely well with intermediate competitions I did wonder whether he might be a bit limited at advanced level. I rode him in one advanced class at the South of England but pulled him up halfway round; he had not actually made a mistake but I could feel he was losing confidence the further he went. Because his dressage was so good, and since he was more than capable of intermediate cross-country tracks, I decided to keep him for a while as a fun horse. When you are trying to make your mark as an event rider it does no harm at all to have a horse that you know you can pull out and win on at a certain level – it keeps adding points and prize money to your name, and this all helps to keep your sponsor interested and

Left: In 1986 the Carphone Group bought a new lorry for Mary, and sponsored the whole team. This photogaph was taken on a freezing cold day in Salcombe Regis early in the year, shortly before George (Diver's Rock) was put down. (Left to right) Arthur, Tina, George, Mary, Boris, Silver, Annie and Max

Right: How the mighty are fallen! Seb Coe cleans Mary's boots at Breda

Far right: A slight problem for Mary and Max at Locko Intermediate Championships in 1987. Mary is far too far in front of the movement from the start; had her weight been further back Max might have been able to keep up in front. *He* didn't actually fall – but Mary did!

enjoying the sport. Max won the Windsor three-day event the following spring, and then we went to Breda in Holland. There he performed a truly sensational dressage test – he was awarded the full ten marks for his extended trot, and that was by a German judge! I still think it was one of the best dressage tests I have ever ridden.

'But by the following year, much as it was fun to go out and win one-day events with him, I was finding that I really needed to devote more time to the younger horses in the yard – by this time I had eight or nine horses to ride. We had always thought

that Max would make a brilliant Junior team horse, as their championships are of intermediate standard and therefore of a level which he could cope with very well, so he was sold to a Junior rider who gained a great deal of experience on him. And when she wanted to move on to greater things he was sold to a lady who still has him, and adores him; he is competing at elementary level with her in pure dressage, and enters the occasional pre-novice one-day event where he runs non-competitively because he is over-qualified; but he gives his rider a great sense of achievement, nonetheless.'

Before Mary's name became synonymous with the King horses, there was one very special horse which first brought her to prominence as a rider: ***DIVER'S ROCK.***

'I was looking through the *Horse and Hound* "For Sale" advertisements to see if there was anything suitable that I could afford – I had £3,500 to spend having just sold another horse, and this particular advertisement for an ex-show horse caught my eye. He was described as an eight-year-old, 17.2hh dark bay gelding. He had been to Wembley as a show horse, but his temperament was not really suited to competing at that level and so he was bought by Jennie Loriston-Clarke who took him to medium level in pure dressage – but again, his temperament prevented him from progressing any further. He was then sold as a hack to a young girl who lived in the New Forest; and because she was intending to emigrate, he was for sale.

'I fell in love with him as soon as I saw him; he was in show condition and so looked absolutely massive, but he was a lovely, big-moving horse. His owner rode him for me on the flat, and then I asked to see him over a jump; and I shall always remember her turning to me in horror and saying, "No fear, you can jump him, but I'm not!" So I trotted him towards a tiny little jump, and as soon as he saw it he just tore at it, and knocked the poles flying. But I was so overcome by his beauty that it never really occurred to me that he might not do the job I wanted – basically, I just couldn't believe that I might be able to buy such a beautiful horse with my limited budget.

'Once he was home I rode him every day over poles on the ground, gradually building up to tiny fences, until one day he just settled; it was as though he finally realised that there was nothing to worry about, and he just got on with the job in hand. I don't believe I even took him cross-country schooling before his first event, at Crookham, but on the day he was fantastic, a real "natural" across country. King William, who came later, proved to be the same: from day one these two horses stayed straight and were bold without getting too strong. After that first event it was as if he had finally found his slot in life, and at last settled to the régime that eventing involved.

'He upgraded to intermediate very quickly, and was a joy to own; he was so safe, sound and bold I just loved riding him. His dressage and cross-country performances were excellent, but we were both a little green in the showjumping. However, his first three-day event was Windsor, where he finished second, and later that year we went on to Boekelo. This was my very first event abroad, and the whole thing was just so exciting; and we finished sixth there, which was just amazing! That year he was presented with a trophy by the BHS for the horse that had won the most points, an occasion which marked my first real recognition as an event rider.

'It was after all this that the Carphone Group first declared an interest in sponsoring us, and Diver's Rock was the horse they chose to support for the following year; this would include our first visit to Badminton. By that time, I finally felt I had made it: I was at Badminton, something I had only ever dreamed of! I never once felt nervous or worried; it was something I had wanted to do for so long that I could only feel the thrill and excitement. Diver's Rock gave me the most brilliant ride across country – as we cleared the most famous fences I remember just grinning from ear to ear and thinking, "Wow! we have just jumped the Vicarage Vee!", or whatever it was.

'We finished 7th, and I also won the Whitbread spurs which were presented to the best rider under twenty-five years old. In those days it was a set of gold spurs presented by Her Majesty the Queen. On top of all that we had been noticed by the selectors. I did not understand anything about selection committees then, and had never really thought about matters such as teams and championships, so I was quite taken aback when, having cantered out of the showjumping arena on the final day, a stranger handed me a white envelope. When I finally opened it I found an invitation from the senior selection committee to present myself to them the following morning for possible team selection for the 1986 European Championships; there, we were duly long-listed.

'After Badminton, Diver's Rock was slightly unlevel; he had occasionally had trouble with corns so I wasn't unduly worried, but this time it didn't get any better. He went to the Animal Health Trust in Newmarket where Dr Sue Dyson examined him – and they announced that he had very advanced navicular disease. We tried various drug treatments but all to no avail, and finally it was decided to try a revolutionary operating procedure; this involved cutting two of the tissue strands that held the navicular bone in place in the hoof, the tiny amount of movement that this gave the bone being enough to relieve the pressure, or so it was hoped. It did seem to bring him some comfort for a few months, but then he gradually became worse again. Finally, one morning I went to his stable and found him in agony; he was sweaty and colicky and couldn't even put his foot to the floor. My own vet came out to see him, and after discussion with Sue Dyson it was decided that the only option was to have him put down.

'That was a dreadful day – I sent the girls away from the yard for the morning so they were nowhere near. One of the hardest things to come to terms with was the request by the Animal Health Trust to have his front hooves so they could look to see what had gone wrong. This meant keeping them wrapped up in the freezer until we were travelling to an event in that direction, when they came out to collect them. I remember looking at the box that contained his lower leg and hooves and feeling a morbid impulse to open it to see what they looked like; but eventually I decided not to! What they found was a huge abscess in the hoof which had been eating away at everything. They stopped carrying out that particular treatment soon after that.'

Above: Mary with her two main horses early in 1985: Boris and George

Annie on Arthur and Max

'Arthur was a grumpy difficult character but nonetheless I did have a particular liking for him – probably because when he let you do something well, you felt this was a real achievement. He was always very bossy and boisterous, and extremely naughty to hack out: we always rode him in draw-reins to have any hope of holding him. He and I did, however, fall out briefly en route to Boekelo when he decided to bite me on the bosom! Mary came through to the back of the lorry and found me in tears, and I had to confess that my most valuable credentials had nearly disappeared down Arthur's throat!

'On another occasion when he had to be stabled overnight at an event we had been given barley straw as bedding and Arthur ate so much of it that he had colic the next day and could not compete. Now, we always double-check exactly what bedding we are going to be given; at home we use best quality woodshavings, and we always arrange for the same to be provided when we stay away.

'Although Max and Arthur started their competitive lives together, their careers were to be very different. They were both capable of good dressage scores, and could both be a little careless in the showjumping, but across country Arthur was a real professional whereas Max always looked as if he was only doing it because he was being asked to. Arthur had the potential to be a four-star horse, so it was truly heart-breaking that he had to be put down relatively early in his career because of a tendon injury.

'When I went to work for Mary, Max and Arthur were the new novices in the yard. Their first novice event was also my first event as Mary's groom: we went to Aldon and Arthur won his section and Max was fourth, and I thought, "Wow, this is a good game to be in!" They were quite different in character: Max was only a little horse and was very laid back, although he was a confirmed crib-biter; this is a habit where the horse will grasp hold of a fence, or a post, or the manger, and chew at it, perhaps for comfort or because it is bored and frustrated; at one prize-giving Max obviously began to find the proceedings tedious and entertained himself by trying to crib-bite on the head of the person who had been asked to hold him!

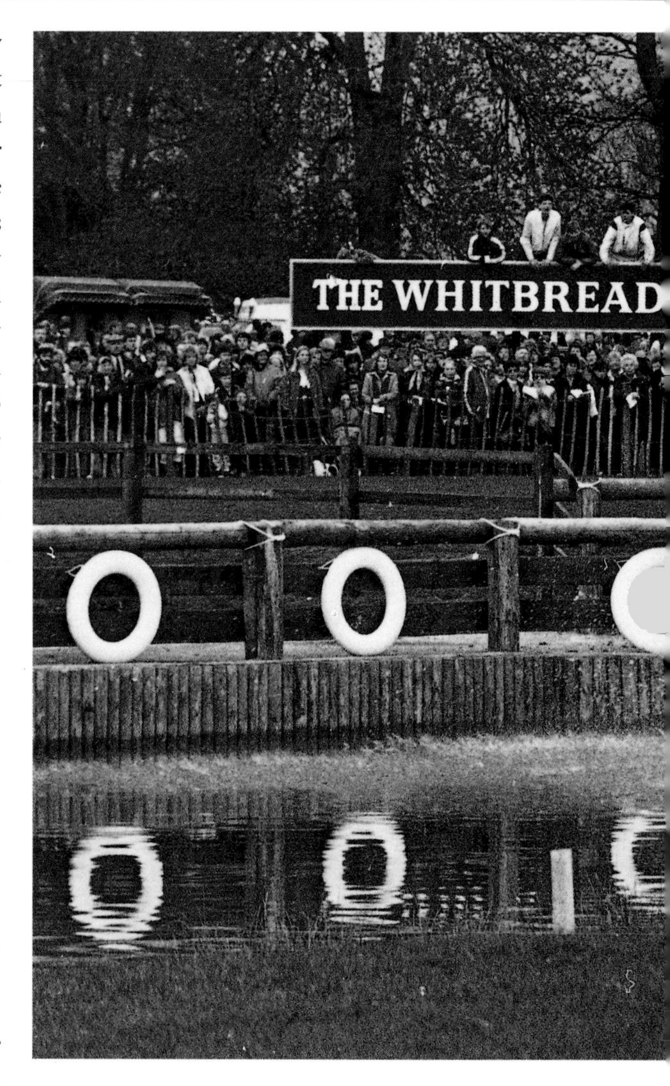

'At home Max was very easy to look after; he was well mannered in the stable and polite to groom, trim and clip; and he was an extremely tidy person – his mane was always in place, and his tail always looked tidy. Once he knew his job he was quite straightforward to ride and compete, too: Mary could concentrate on the other horses and only needed to ride him once, just a few days before a competition, and he would go as well for her as if she rode him every day. He was a good traveller and always settled down quickly into new surroundings; he was never one to worry about what his mates were doing, and if he was content with his circumstances, then nothing else bothered him.'

Gill on Max and George

'One of the early King string was King Max; when Mary bought him he was in poor condition. I was watching him at Tetbury one-day event where his last owner happened to be watching; she announced to her neighbour that he had once been their horse, and related how her daughter had "hunted the backside off him" – and I couldn't stop myself turning round and saying quite sharply, "That's *hardly* something to be proud of!" Feeling sorry for him turned into becoming extremely fond of him. He was only a small horse and was quite shy – I saw him at Longleat Horse Trials in 1996 with the lady who now owns him, and she summed him up well:"He does like his little parties but he also needs to have his own space!"

'He always tried his heart out, and winning Breda three-day event is my best memory of him. That whole week was a succession of really good parties. Max won, and all in all it was a lovely time. Throughout his career he had had his moments in the showjumping – rather like William – but he pulled out all the stops to win on that occasion, and I will always remember it, along with his big floppy ears!

'George was the first horse that I sponsored, but I never got to know him well as his career was so short-lived. I saw him compete once, at Badminton, where he was just *so* impressive across country. I was completely smitten, though I remember thinking he was enormous! It was my first Badminton and my first event horse – and he was *placed*! I still watch his performance on video, and he really was superb; it was tragic that he had to be put down.'

Above: A dream come true: Mary's first Badminton in1985, when she and George came seventh

STABLE NOTES

HUMPRHREY

PERSONAL DETAILS
16.2hh bay gelding, Thoroughbred
Born 1973, breeding unknown
MAIN ACHIEVEMENTS
1st Goodwood 1980
2nd Osberton 1981
144 horse trials points
CHARACTERISTICS
Cheeky, with beautiful big eyes and Roman nose; short-coupled; very inquisitive; banged his door at feed time
LIKES
Going fast across country; having his tongue tickled; weaving (especially at feed time); chewing rugs!
DISLIKES
The dressage and showjumping phases of an event

KING MAX

PERSONAL DETAILS
15.3hh chestnut gelding, ⅞ Thoroughbred type
Born 1979, breeding unknown
MAIN ACHIEVEMENTS
4th Osberton 1986
1st Windsor 1987
1st Breda 1988
337 horse trials points
CHARACTERISTICS
Sweet, gentle little horse; a bit lazy at heart
LIKES
Crib-biting; holidays; sleeping; being pampered
DISLIKES
Very big cross-country fences with big ditches

KING ARTHUR

PERSONAL DETAILS
16.1hh bay gelding, Irish Thoroughbred
Born 1979, breeding unknown
Stable name 'Uncle Arthur'
MAIN ACHIEVEMENTS
1st Osberton 1986
1st Windsor 1987
203 horse trials points
Won many one-day events
CHARACTERISTICS
Kind and gentle, but grumpy in the yard and when travelling; carried his tail crooked; had a long back and short legs; very big mover
LIKES
Cross-country and dressage; baring his teeth to see if you were frightened; biting his stable door while his feed was being prepared
DISLIKES
Showjumping; picking up his back and feet and going backwards, as he was a bit of a 'shiverer'

DIVER'S ROCK

PERSONAL DETAILS
17.2hh dark bay gelding, ⅞ Thoroughbred
Born 1974, by Diver's Gem (15hh flat-race stallion) out of a ¾ TB Irish mare
Stable name 'George'
MAIN ACHIEVEMENTS
2nd Windsor 1984
6th Boekelo 1984
7th Badminton 1985
283 horse trials points
Won The Calcutta Light Horse Trophy in 1984 for the highest number of points
CHARACTERISTICS
An absolute gentleman, angelic in the stable and to ride; was an ex-show horse with Roger Stack; tremendous presence
LIKED
Galloping at speed over big fences; dressage – he was a beautiful mover
DISLIKED
Parked cars with engine running; crowds of noisy people; men, especially vets!

The STARS

Star Appeal, aged five, going brilliantly cross-country at his first event, at Llanfechain, in 1990

Boris is not the sort of horse to take to retirement easily. He came to Mary as a five-year-old in 1984, and is a member of that élite group of horses who have amassed over 1,000 horse trials points. He spent his life with Mary being pampered and fussed over, always the centre of attention; he was the first to whinny to anyone entering the yard, always wanted to be first on the lorry, and was always impatient to get off at the other end! At the end of the 1995 season Boris moved to live with Paula Lee, a young rider based at Lympstone, Devon, where Mary and Annie can still keep an eye on him. In return for being thoroughly spoilt he will compete in riding club dressage and showjumping classes.

BORIS

STABLE NOTES

PERSONAL DETAILS

16.3hh bay gelding, ⅞ Thoroughbred

Born 1979, by Rapid Pass (TB) out of Miss Mandy II (hunter)

MAIN ACHIEVEMENTS

2nd Badminton 1989

3rd Badminton 1990

1st Gatcombe British Open Championships 1990

4th Burghley 1991

He earned 1,207 horse trials points in his career, and was placed in 75 of 85 competitions entered

CHARACTERISTICS

Very extrovert, fun-loving and attention-seeking; easily recognisable in competitions because of his swishing tail; when nervous or excited his bottom lip wobbles

LIKES

Food (he constantly thinks of his stomach!); attention; going travelling (always rushes up the horse-box ramp, begging to be off to another 'party'!)

DISLIKES

Diets; pigs; being trimmed with scissors

Although Boris was not Mary's first advanced horse (her first ride at Badminton, for example, was on Diver's Rock), he is really the founder member of her team of event horses, and the one that most people remember. He was the first to sport the famous 'King' prefix, as David King (then Mary's boyfriend) helped her to buy him; and he

is the horse who Mary feels has taught her the most. He is an adorable character: he loves attention, and has always been treated to plenty; he has huge brown eyes that just beg forgiveness; and as Mary is the first to point out, he was very tolerant of many of the early mistakes she made with him.

Mary found Boris in 1984:

'This was before I was being sponsored by anyone, and David offered to help me buy another horse. Boris was advertised in *Horse and Hound* magazine, and had been bred for showing – he had been shown successfully as a youngster, but had not matured into the top-class show horse that his owner, Geoffrey Buckingham Bawden, had hoped for. I just saw this head with huge kind eyes and big ears, looking at me over the stable door, and fell in love with him straightaway! Being in a showyard he was obviously beautifully presented, but what I really liked was the purposeful, almost bossy way in which he marched out of the stable. Although he hadn't really been introduced to jumping, I trotted him down to a small cavalletti, which he attacked eagerly. He was obviously naive in that he didn't really know quite how to handle himself, but he showed that he was kind and eager to please.'

Boris came to Mary's yard in the autumn of that year, and spent the winter being prepared for his first novice season. 'He was quite overweight and this made him rather stuffy to gallop. But he did a few hunter trials and I hunted him in an effort to teach him to gallop and open himself out, and this helped him enormously. It was interesting to see how it also helped his flatwork generally; after a season's hunting he could produce an extravagant extended trot!'

The opening event of the 1985 season was at Penzance where, in order to encourage more people to make the long trip down to Cornwall, the organisers held an event on the Friday, and another on the Saturday. Although Mary acknowledged that two consecutive events was a lot to expect of a young horse, she was also keen to capitalise on the opportunity to build up some experience quickly.

Page 30: A kiss for Boris after his dressage test at Badminton 1991

Boris was second in one event and first in the other, earning himself 11 horse trials points (halfway to intermediate) in one weekend!

Despite this sudden success there were still some problems:

'Boris was still very inexperienced and, looking back on it, I didn't know as much about fitness and keeping a horse off his forehand when galloping as I do now. So he was probably still a little overweight and could have been fitter. On top of that, when we went across country he tended to be very heavy on my hand, which is a sign that he was unbalanced and too much on his forehand. This was also revealed in his dressage as he was very reliant on my hand to support him and, right from the start, had the habit of swishing his tail and working with his ears flat back, a characteristic which proved very expensive when he competed later at Badminton.'

But despite all this Boris continued to be placed in competitions and, more significantly, he won a very important admirer during his first season. Early in the year Mary had been awarded her first sponsorship contract. The fast-growing Carphone Group had approached the Horse Trials Committee with a view to offering sponsorship to event riders. Mary's name was among those considered and selected, and she was offered support for herself and Diver's Rock, with whom she was about to attempt her first Badminton. A few weeks before the great event she rode Boris at the Portman horse trials, watched by her proud new sponsors Graham and Gill Thomas (now Robinson). Mary recalls, 'I was really keen to impress my sponsors but managed to see a really bad stride in the showjumping and had the next three fences down, which was very unusual for Boris. But Gill just thought he was wonderful – in her eyes we could do no wrong – and she fell completely and utterly in love with him.' And so the Carphone Group's sponsorship was extended to cover King Boris as well.

The weekend after Mary's successful Badminton debut (where they finished seventh and were long-listed for the European Championships) she rode Boris in his first intermediate event, and she was more nervous about this than she had been about tackling the daunting Badminton course. 'Getting to Badminton had been my dream for so long that I savoured and enjoyed every second. But then to ride baby Boris, who still seemed so inexperienced, around an intermediate course was nerve-racking! He had to go in the Open Intermediate section, too, which meant he was competing against advanced horses as well, and yet he still finished second. He attempted his first three-day event, Osberton, at the end of his first season, and I had really high hopes because everything had gone so well up till then.'

Mary and Boris had their first major upset at Osberton, at what should have been the highlight of their first season together. Mary, with her discerning honesty in these matters, took full blame for what happened.

'I just saw this head with huge kind eyes and big ears, and fell in love with him straightaway!'

'Basically I was going at too fast a pace on the cross-country. In those days I made the same mistake as a lot of inexperienced riders, and that is to go too fast for the degree of accuracy that I possessed. We came whizzing round a corner towards what I thought was a very simple steeplechase-type fence, although it had a brush apron in front of it, and a slight drop the other side. I went for a very long stride; Boris decided he couldn't clear the fence like that so he banked it (put his feet back down on top of the fence, and then jumped off again). I fell off but, worse than that, a splinter of wood from the fence had gone into Boris' knee. It was an awful experience; we took him back to the stable but his knee was hurting so much that he actually got colic from the pain. Until the tranquillisers and painkillers took effect there was nothing we could do to help him.'

Miraculously the splinter had not damaged the joint capsule, and over the winter months Boris made a full recovery. He came out the following season, seven years old, feeling better than ever; his confidence did not seem to have been affected at all. The aim of that season was to do the 2-star three-day event in Breda, Holland:

'It was only my second foreign event, and again we all set out in great excitement and with high hopes. But when I walked the course the fences

Above left: Mary proudly showing off her new young horse early in 1985

Disaster at the Normandy Bank. Mary and Boris approached on a holding stride, and rather than jumping onto the bank and bouncing off it Boris tried to put in a little stride on top, bringing him too close to the rail. Being so genuine he tried to jump it, but fell straight over it; incredibly he was on his feet, unscathed, straightaway. Mary was unconscious for twenty mintues (the second photograph shows Lucinda Green on Shannagh being stopped on the course), came round without even a headache and wanted to ride Cuthbert later the same day, but wasn't allowed to

looked huge; I was especially worried about the gaping ditches as Boris was always quite a careful horse and a little wary of big holes in the ground. But the steeplechase phase seemed to open him out and to make him really bold, and he went extremely well across country to finish fourth.

'At his first event of the autumn season he was leading after the dressage and showjumping. The ground was very dry and hard and I was a little worried about running him across country; but Mum, who is normally quite impartial about these things, was really keen for us to go out and win it – Boris deserved it, after all. He did win, but he also strained his tendon which meant our season ended there.

'The following year he was fit and well and we went out to do the 3-star Stockholm three-day event. But once more I made a major error on the cross-country. I was still riding Boris in a snaffle and had not really appreciated that this was not a strong enough bit for him. He still had a tendency to lean on my hand, and as a consequence he was difficult to shorten up and balance in front of his fences. So once again I went on a long stride to a very wide parallel; Boris came down on the back rail and, despite hitting himself very hard, seemed to be all-right. I got back on and, all credit to him, he just picked up and carried on round the rest of the course. But he stiffened up overnight and we did not attempt to bring him out for the final phase.'

'I was just so angry...I was the only one to slip up.'

Mary is very rarely seen with anything less than a broad smile on her face, win or lose, but she admits to shutting herself in her room and crying for most of that night.

'I was just so angry that I had made such a mistake. I had been part of the British team at the event – there was Ginny Leng, John Evans and Rachel Hunt, all with promising young horses – and I was the only one to slip up. Looking back I can never thank Boris enough for his courage and confidence. He always bounced back from whatever happened, and never held it against me. He gave me the chance to learn so much, and yet he was still learning himself. It just emphasises what a kind, genuine competitor he was. True to form he bounced back in the autumn and won on his first outing, before going on to tackle the 4-star Burghley event. The dressage was the phase we both found difficult, but he was jumping brilliantly. I managed to avoid making any major errors and he produced a double clear which won him eighth place.

'With this encouraging performance behind us we were ready for Badminton the following spring. Our dressage had started to improve now that I was getting help from Ferdi Eilberg, and I was really excited about tackling Badminton again. It seemed a long time since I had had my first ride there on Diver's Rock in 1985. I was first to go across country and we were going great guns until the run down to the Normandy Bank. Boris was starting to feel tired and heavy and, having still not fully learned my lesson from the mistake in Stockholm, I was allowing him to rely on my hand for support. I wanted to shorten him up in front of the bank but with all his weight on his forehand I was having to pull with all my strength just to check him back. I ended up holding him all the way into the fence so we arrived with too little impulsion for what was needed. He tried to get us out of the muddle by putting in a little stride on top of the bank, but this took him too close to the rail on the top and we turned a somersault. This time he escaped injury, but I was knocked out cold.

'By 1989, when Boris was ten, and we returned to Badminton once more, we were far more in control of our destiny. I was really beginning to enjoy the dressage training and as a result Boris was improving all the time. And I had started to ride him in a vulcanite pelham across country, which made all the difference to our performance. He was lying fourth after the dressage, was clear on the cross-country and produced a clear round in the final showjumping phase. We finished second behind Ginny Leng and Master Craftsman. I always look on that Badminton as the one that Boris should have won; at a three-day event your dressage is judged by the three members of the ground jury, and your score is an average of their marks. Two of the judges put him in first place but the third judge, who had never seen him compete, placed him thirty-first because he regarded his tail swishing and flattened ears as a resistance. After the event he apologised as he had not realised that that was just part of Boris' way of going and, in fact, he marked him more generously than the other judges the following year. But the margin between winning and losing was so tight that had he been kinder to him in the dressage Boris would have won the event.

'The judge regarded Boris' tail swishing and flattened ears as a resistance.'

'By this time Boris was a very consistent performer and was winning many advanced classes. We were third at Badminton the following year, and went into team training in preparation for the World Equestrian Games. We were officially there as first reserves which meant if any of the four main choices had a setback then we could go. On his actual form he easily deserved a place in the team, but in the eyes of the selectors he was not the ideal type of event horse; they preferred the full Thoroughbred type. Right up until the afternoon that the team flew out there was just a glimmer of hope for Boris, as there was some concern about the soundness of one of the team horses. But the selectors satisfied themselves that the horse was OK, and Boris was left behind. It was no consolation that one of the horses did in fact have to retire because of lameness.'

'... that's just the type of horse he was; I made a mistake, and he forgave it and just carried on...'

There was, however, comfort to come in the shape of Boris' popular win in the British Open Championships at Gatcombe that autumn; and Burghley was also a great success for both Boris and King Cuthbert, Boris' regular partner in crime. After the cross-country phase Bertie and Boris were lying first and third respectively, but both had the last showjump down and so dropped to second and fourth places. Mary admits that she made the classic mistake of coming to the last fence on a long flat stride and just assuming they would clear it as they were both good jumpers.

'Finding ourselves in the lead after the dressage at Badminton the following year, I was convinced that we were going to win this time. Boris was travelling easily around the course as we approached the Lake. Here there was a bounce into the water to be negotiated, but I had not really appreciated that the distance was riding very long. I didn't attack it with quite enough pace which meant we jumped into the bounce a bit short. Boris had to really stretch to clear the rail out, but just caught his girth on it which made him land very steeply in the water. He stayed on his feet, but I was tipped off over his shoulder. I was so bitterly disappointed that when we were reunited I could hardly decide whether or not to carry on beyond the next fence, which I did jump if only to restore our confidence. The decision was made for me when, having slowed to a hand canter, I still couldn't find a gap in the string by which to leave

RIGHT: Mary displays a brilliant half-pass (who needs Boris?) after leading the dressage at Badminton in 1991

the course. So I thought we might as well carry on – Boris was happy to oblige in spite of the fact that the next fence was the daunting Coffin. But that's just the type of horse he was; I made a mistake, and he forgave it and just carried on, ready for the next challenge. But that night he was lame; he had damaged his suspensory ligament sufficiently severely that it ended his three-day eventing career. On the advice of Sue Dyson, an equine specialist at the Animal Health Trust, we carried on competing him at one-day level, at which he was consistently successful, once he had fully recovered. In his career he competed in 85 events, and was placed in 75 of them!'

At this stage in a horse's career it can be difficult for a rider to decide on exactly the right moment for him to retire. But Boris, being Boris, let Mary know when he had had enough. In the spring of 1995, when he was sixteen, he won the Advanced section at Cornbury; but as the year went on, and the ground got harder, Mary noticed that Boris was finding the work tougher and she knew that the time had come.

Left: Mary on Boris, with Cuthbert, 'Annie's gift horse'

Above: Boris, with tail swishing hard as usual, flies off the Fairbank Bounce at Badminton in 1989

Annie on Boris

Boris' first eventing season was also Annie's first season in her role as Mary's groom. As she and Boris were very much the 'new kids on the block' she has always felt a great affection for him. 'Boris was always really good to do; he loved the fuss and attention that being an event horse involved. We both had our first foreign trip when Boris competed at Breda, and I can remember Mary suggesting that I lead Boris back after the dressage,

as he was always so pleased with himself when he finished his test that he could get very naughty. As it was I would probably have been safer on his back; I ended up swinging around on the end of his lead rope while he gaily attempted to pummel me into the ground! It was one of the very few times when he did not behave like a gentleman!'

Unfortunately for Annie, Mary's memories of Annie's first trip abroad have more to do with the social whirl attached to the event; as Annie took to the dance floor, determined to make the most of the evening, she twirled with such gusto that one of her stiletto heels snapped off; undaunted, she continued to dance all night with one leg a good three inches shorter than the other!

Boris' win at the British Open at Gatcombe stands out in Annie's mind as one of the very special moments in her life.

'After the disappointment of not being chosen for the European Championships it was just so good to see him achieve such a well deserved outright win. Gill Robinson [née Thomas] and I were in tears watching him romp round. The time was really tight and, as the competition is run in reverse order of merit, he was the last to go, and had to get a good time in order to hold on to his lead. He never looked particularly fast across country – in fact, with his tail swishing furiously he often made it look like hard work – and we could see Captain Mark Phillips shaking his head, convinced that he wouldn't beat the clock – but he did it!

'At home in Devon people started to take far more notice of Mary and the yard after that. On the event circuit itself Boris had already picked up quite a following as he was easy to recognise on the cross-country with his tail propelling him along. He had a big fan club whose attention he adored; he would push his nose into the midst of everybody, which they loved as they thought he was saying "Hello" – in fact he was probably trying to look for Polo mints, knowing Boris!

'Poor Boris loved his food and was a very good doer, so he was on an almost permanent diet which didn't please him at all. But he was such a contented character that he could get fat on fresh air. When he was given his food he always took one huge mouthful, far more than he could swallow, and would then spill it all over the place in an effort to gulp it all down. He would then spend hours searching out every last morsel from his bedding.

'He loved everything connected with sport – the travelling, staying in different stables, and particularly the jumping. He always gave the impression that he condescended to perform the dressage in order to be allowed to get on and jump. He was not naturally fast across country and had to work hard to get a good time, and yet he was always as pleased as Punch with himself when he completed a course. Had he been a person he would have been a non-stop party-goer, and always good company.

'It was really sad when he retired and left the yard – being such an extrovert character meant that the gap he left behind was far more than just an empty stable – but it was far better for him to go to another home where he will still be the kingpin. Had he stayed with us he would have been really upset to find the younger horses gradually taking over from him.'

Above: Annie's little joke: a 'welcome home' reminder of Mary and Boris' crash into the Lake at Badminton, in 1991

Gill on Boris

Gill Robinson, Boris' part-owner and Mary's long-standing supporter and sponsor pays tribute to her all-time favourite by describing him as 'the most brilliant horse that never quite made it to the top'. One of the biggest disappointments during her long involvement with Mary was that Boris was never chosen to represent his country; in the eyes of his owners and rider he was more than good enough, and deserved the opportunity of proving himself worthy for selection, which came close in 1990 when he was first reserve for the European Championships.

Boris was a five-year-old novice when Gill first saw him. Even now she cannot quite explain what it was about him that captured her heart so completely:

'He was such a round, roly-poly little horse; he had huge eyes and ears and was a brilliant bright bay, and I just had a gut feeling that he was going to be something special.

'Boris' greatest attribute was his huge heart and his devotion to Mary; if she asked him to do something, as far as he was concerned he just had to do it. He always gave of his best, and had the ability to lift everyone's spirits. He adored the attention that came his way – he was convinced that every single spectator at Badminton had come just to see him, and he would grow in stature and produce his best performance for them. Take him to a cold, windy one-day event where there was nobody to watch him in the dressage, and he would shuffle round like an old donkey! He taught Mary a tremendous amount because, by her own admission, he always forgave her her mistakes and would go one better next time.'

Like Annie, Gill's happiest memory of Boris' career is his win at the British Open at Gatcombe. 'I watched him going over the first three fences and I knew he was going to win. Throughout his career a lot of people were sceptical about him and felt he wasn't quite good enough or fast enough, and I could hear the commentators expressing some doubts about his speed on this occasion, but Boris and I knew better!'

Gill remembers Boris as being in complete charge of the yard at home – 'he always gave the impression that everything was run entirely for his benefit' – and has amusing memories of one ride on him.

'I was determined to do everything properly and not let him down. So I mounted in the yard – and he immediately marched off into the open barn. When I ticked him off Mary just called over "It's alright, Boris doesn't want you to have to stand outside in the rain!" We set off for our hack, and all went well until we turned for home. As he broke into a jog I realised that my brakes might not be quite as effective as they had been on the way out, but that was fine by Mary – "Boris always likes to jog home." Back in the yard once more I tried to hang on to him as I unsaddled him, but he pushed past me and went to drink from the trough to a chorus of "Don't worry Gill, Boris always does that!" By the end of the day I was left in no doubt as to who was King of that yard!

'I miss him dreadfully now that he's retired; it's just not the same now that he's no longer watching who comes into the yard. But he ended his career sound, happy and successful, and he's bringing happiness to someone else now, who spoils him rotten. Life has turned out just the way he likes it!'

Above: Boris in retirement: meeting two new friends, Shire horses Diamond and Hazel and with his field companion, Jim

Greenham

King Cuthbert was bought for Mary by her sponsors The Carphone Group early in 1986. Except for Humphrey, he is the only 'ready-made' horse that Mary has ever had, in that he already had intermediate points

CUTHBERT

when he came to Mary as a nine-year-old.

'After Diver's Rock went lame and had to be put down, I was without a top-level horse. I had a few novices as well as King Boris who had just upgraded to intermediate, but I didn't have a horse to compete on at the highest level. My sponsors were obviously keen for me to ride at advanced level, and as the overall sponsors of the Bramham three-day event, they particularly wanted me to have a ride there.'

STABLE NOTES

PERSONAL DETAILS

16.1hh bay gelding

Born 1977, Irish bred by Zolferine

Stable name 'Bert'

MAIN ACHIEVEMENTS

1st Bramham 1986

2nd Bramham 1988

7th Badminton 1990

2nd Burghley 1990

575 horse trial points

CHARACTERISTICS

Whinnies softly but continually at feed time; *always* stales when he starts eating a new net of hay; a typical red-head, as he gets excited easily; has plenty of *joie de vivre*, even in his old age!

LIKES

Loved competing and everything associated with an event; although he is turned out every day he still finds it wildly exciting, and he bends at the knees to roll even before the headcollar is off, then trots off, tail in air, squealing and bucking

DISLIKES

Titbits! Declines Polos and carrots, though – to avoid offence – could just about manage a piece of apple. Also *hates* mopeds

King Cuthbert had been taken rapidly through novice to intermediate level in Ireland. He had completed the Punchestown three-day event as a seven-year-old, and had then been bought by Bernice Cuthbert of Aston Park Stud. She had him for a year, during which time she rode him at advanced level but took him very quietly in an attempt to settle down and improve his technique. Cuthbert has previously been galloped and jumped very fast; he was a real hot-head, and although he had had some success he had also had a few falls as a result of his over-enthusiasm.

'Cuthbert, in his enthusiasm jumped out before they said "Go" and we set off full tilt for the first fence'

Mary had only a few one-day events in which to get to know her new horse before facing the pressure of competing at Bramham for her sponsors.

'It was certainly a different experience riding a horse which had been produced and competed by someone else. It made it harder to know how it would react in certain situations – but equally it was good to sit on a horse that knew what it was supposed to be doing, rather than always being the one trying to teach it what the job was about. However, before Bramham I rode at King's Somborne advanced, and we had a real purler of a fall. It was at a very simple fence where I saw a long stride – but Cuthbert disagreed and put in a very short one, hit the fence and we turned a somersault. Despite this we went to Bramham, and won it! As well as Cuthbert I was also riding a horse called Silverstone there, for someone else. On the final day Cuthbert was lying first and Silverstone was third, and I was allowed to jump Silverstone further down the order to give me time to warm up on Cuthbert. It so happened that Silverstone had a clear round which put him in the lead, so no matter what happened on Cuthbert I had already won the event! Luckily, though, Cuthbert also jumped clear and so *he* won it, and Silverstone was second.

'In fact, things had not gone as smoothly as they might have done on cross-country day. To begin with, I had had flu before Bramham and did not realise that I had lost weight; I had never before had to ride with a weightcloth, and had gone down to the start as usual for the official weigh-in, only to find I was underweight. We didn't actually possess a weightcloth, so I had to rush back to the stable to try and borrow one. I couldn't find anyone I knew, so ended up just taking Tiny Clapham's from her lorry – I felt dreadful about it, although I did know for sure that she wouldn't need it till much later on in the day. It was then a rush to fit it under the saddle and to weigh in again. When we arrived at the start of phase A they had already counted us down to go, so I knew we had some time to catch up. We cantered the first part of the roads and tracks to try and make it up, which we managed to do before we got to phase B, the steeplechase. We went into the start-box but then Cuthbert, in his enthusiasm, jumped out before they said "Go" and we set off full tilt for the first fence. It took all my strength to pull him up so that we could be restarted, which was the rule then if you had a false start – now they just add time penalties to your score. So again I knew we had time to make up; but Cuthbert demonstrated his speed by successfully completing the steeplechase inside the time. He gave me a superb ride across country, although in hindsight I now appreciate that I was still at the stage of probably going too fast to be safe. I was still learning the principles of the sport, and thought that speed was vital; but this was when I didn't have the experience always to judge the fences safely when galloping at such a pace. But on this occasion our very fast time helped us to win overall.

'At Gatcombe later that year, however, speed was indeed our undoing. We were in with a chance of winning, and although I knew I really needed to take him in hand a bit more, Cuthbert had already picked up too much speed. I remember trying to slow him down, but the more you fought him the faster he tried to go; he would throw his head around

'He landed on me, and as he struggled up my foot was still caught in the stirrup...'

Page 42: Annie and her 'main man' Cuthbert

and go sideways towards his fences. To cut a long story short, we made a mistake coming into the coffin: he slipped just before taking off, which took him too close to the first rail and we cartwheeled over it. He landed on me, and as he struggled up my foot was still caught in the stirrup so my body was wrenched round, and this strained my groin muscle badly. Mum was watching on a neighbour's television, and wasn't too worried as she could see me smile as I was put into the ambulance. But when I rang her from the hospital, initially to say I was all right, I suddenly felt a real stab of pain: in fact I had some internal bleeding, so all Mum heard was me screaming in agony and saying I had to go, which was far worse then if I hadn't rung her at all!

'Cuthbert's next main event was the Rotherfield three-day event, where he was runner-up to Ginny Leng and Griffin. That was not without its excitement, too: because of my groin injury Annie had been busy keeping Cuthbert fit while I recuperated, but I hadn't realised how much fitness *I* had lost; I was so tired that I nearly fell off going over the last few fences on the cross-country!

'Boekelo three-day event was the highlight of the following season. It is always such a fun event, but it was nearly a non-starter for Cuthbert. I had been riding him about on the first day and had found a lovely big field to work in. But whilst we were trotting round, his foot went down a rabbit hole. It gave us a real jolt, but he seemed quite all right, so I carried on working him, then stabled him again to wait for the first horse inspection. He was always such a tough, sound horse that I never did much with him before a vets' inspection – and so it was a dreadful shock when, as he trotted up in front of the ground jury, I could hear from his hoofbeats that he was lame. Fortunately they did not eliminate us immediately but put us in the holding box. I walked him round energetically, and by the time he trotted up again he was sound. He must have just stiffened up while he was in the stable earlier on – but it taught me always to walk and trot my horses up before presenting them to the ground jury so I know sooner if there is a problem that needs dealing with. Cuthbert went really well to finish seventh.

'By the following year, 1988, I felt that we were ready to tackle Badminton. Both Boris and Cuthbert were entered and they both produced good dressage performances: Boris was fourth, and Cuthbert was a couple of places behind. But poor Cuthbert was dogged by more bad luck, because I rode Boris first and had a bad fall with him at the Normandy bank. Because I had been knocked out I wasn't allowed to ride my second horse – so there was Cuthbert, fit and raring to go, but confined to his stable! To give him a run we took him back to Bramham where he finished second, narrowly beaten by King's Jester and Jane Thelwall.

'In 1989 Cuthbert at last had a chance to tackle Badminton. We had had a good build-up during the spring, winning the advanced class at Brigstock. Despite his highly excitable temperament Cuthbert contained himself remarkably well

Above: Cuthbert won Bramham in 1986, the first full year of Carphone Group sponsorship. The company sponsored the event, and with impeccable timing Mary took first and second places

to produce a good dressage test – but yet again on the cross-country his exuberance and my inexperience were our undoing: on the approach to the double of white rails in front of the famous Badminton Lake, I tried to collect him a bit more to help prepare him for the upright fences to come, but he resisted by throwing his head around, making it very difficult to hold a good rhythm and see a stride. I held him for one stride too many, and this put him so close to the fence that he couldn't clear it, and we both fell. He completed the rest of the course really well, but our fall and the time faults we collected dropped us to last place at the end of cross-country day!

'Ironically, Cuthbert's most successful year turned out to be his retirement year.'

'Ironically, Cuthbert's most successful year turned out to be his retirement year. In 1990 he achieved his long-overdue clear round at Badminton to finish seventh, a well deserved result for him. We went to Burghley that autumn where he gave me a fantastic cross-country round, putting us into the lead going into the final showjumping phase. I was also second on Boris at this stage. Unbelievably I jumped clear with both horses up to the final fence, which I had down with *both* of them – I think it was just a case of breathing a sigh of relief one fence too soon! Cuthbert finished second and Boris dropped to fourth. This was Cuthbert's biggest success to date, but although he was only thirteen, I made the decision to retire him. He had a brilliant one-day event record, he was a fantastic cross-country horse and he really was very talented on the flat, but he often let himself down by just getting far too excited. Preparing him for a three-day event meant really and truly drilling him day after day to get him sufficiently settled to produce an acceptable test on the day. I began to feel that it was unfair to have to work and pressure him so much in order to get a good result. I also knew that he had worked very hard as a youngster when he was competed in Ireland, so although he wasn't too old by

Top: Cuthbert executes a super halt after a very naughty test
Above: Annie and Cuthbert in retirement have a great time hunting

any means to carry on, he did have a great many miles on his personal clock. He had always been Annie's favourite horse, and nothing could have pleased me more than Gill Robinson's decision to give him to Annie once he retired.

'Cuthbert didn't really respond to my usual tried and tested methods of settling a horse before its dressage test. As a rule, I will take an excitable horse out for a hack if time allows, and then put him back in the stable. He might be lunged before I ride him to warm him up for the test. Sometimes I ride one warm-up, put the horse away and then bring him out again about twenty minutes before the test for a final ride in – but none of this worked with Cuthbert! Every time you brought him out he was just as excited as the first time. So eventually I simply had to drill him for so long that his excess energy wore off. This didn't matter so much at a one-day event, but it was a worrying thing to have to do at a three-day event, when normally you try to conserve all the horse's energy for speed and endurance day. But Cuthbert always managed to find something extra to see him through the cross-country and showjumping phases.

'I well remember the first year he went to Badminton. During the afternoon of the day before his dressage test I was working him in with all the other riders. One by one they finished and headed

Above: A perfect bascule at Brigstock, Cuthbert's last run before Badminton in 1988

back to the stables, but I was still there with Cuthbert, working under the watchful eye of my trainer Ferdi Eilberg. Cuthbert had so much energy that I just kept working him in canter, which is usually the best pace for settling an over-energetic horse. There was no need to practise any of the movements as Cuthbert could do them all beautifully: it was simply a case of getting him to relax. We just kept cantering round the arena and practising our entrance, as it was always just as you turned down the centre line that Cuthbert liked to let everybody know just how pleased he was to be performing by squealing and jiggling one way or the other. So that evening we kept on doing it over and over again, cantering on either rein, turning down the centre or three-quarter line until he did it without being silly. At one stage I really felt that we were going to be there all night! On the day itself I would usually take him for a hack round, and maybe let him have a jump or two to help get rid of some of his energy, but other than that it was down to just drilling his exuberance out of him.

'Cuthbert liked to let everyone know how pleased he was to be performing by squealing and jiggling...'

'Sometimes we tried surprise tactics! At Rotherfield, where he was eventually runner-up to Ginny Leng, I worked him for ages without getting the desired result. So I put him back in the stable, and asked Annie to bring him out, tacked up, just as the horse before us started its test. Annie could hardly believe what she was being told to do, as this gave us only about five minutes to prepare him – but it worked! He was in the arena and had started his test before he realised where he was, and he produced one of his best tests ever. But then at Gatcombe one year he was so appalling that the only people he impressed were the spectators, who found his bucking and squealing highly entertaining. But usually the preliminary hard work was repaid with a good test, although as he got older it seemed a high price to pay for success – hence the decision to retire him when he was thirteen.'

Annie's love affair with Cuthbert

'I clearly remember Cuthbert's arrival in the yard: this wild-looking chestnut horse arrived one day, and it was just my luck that Mary was off to a competition the next day so I was left to take him for a hack. I set off round what we call the "Donkey Block" which is the quietest ride we have – but Cuthbert found it all wildly exhilarating! After Boris, who could be a little lazy on a hack, Cuthbert's squealing, running sideways and prancing on the spot took a bit of getting used to! But we survived, and once I realised that his worst wasn't really too bad I just loved riding him. Although he would jump up and down on the spot you knew he wouldn't rear right up, and when he squealed and bucked it was never with the intention of unseating you. Sitting on him was quite like sitting in an armchair, and he always carried his head very high which made you feel safe. I think I loved him as much as I did because he was always in Boris' shadow. I knew that Boris was Mary's favourite, and Gill Robinson's too, and I always felt a bit sorry for Bert, because he really meant well – he just couldn't contain his excitement. I was so pleased when he was second at Burghley – it wasn't so much where he came, but that fact that just for once he had been able to beat Boris.

'Cuthbert was also my favourite because I think we are very alike in character – we both like to have a good time at parties! And despite his over-enthusiasm when he was being ridden, he was really charming in the stable. He was always very aware of where you were, and would be horrified if he accidentally bumped into you. He would move over whenever you asked him, and would wait until you tied his haynet up before attacking it. He was so kind that you could turn him out with any other horse and know that he wouldn't hurt it or wind it up.

'It didn't take anybody very long to realise that Cuthbert was my "main man", and in fact the first year that he and Boris went to Badminton, Tina decided that we should do the honourable thing: so they held a marriage ceremony for Cuthbert and I, and every year since Tina has sent us an anniversary card!

'I knew during the run-up to Burghley that

Cuthbert was going to be retired that year. I didn't really feel it was my place to ask what they would do with him, but I remember going on and on to Tina about how things would never be the same once Bert left the yard. It came as a complete surprise when, at Gatcombe that autumn, Gill Robinson turned to me and asked if I would like to have him as a gift. I didn't know what to say – I wanted to say "yes" so badly, but I knew only too well that it would be expensive to keep him, and I couldn't help wondering how I could fit him in with work and everything else. But Mary and Gill had thought of all that, and Cuthbert was allowed to stay in the yard; and even to this day, Gill still helps pay for his shoeing and suchlike. I am just so, *so* grateful to them both for enabling things to work out as they have. Hunting is my main love, and although the first few days on Cuthbert were hair-raising because he found it even more exciting than eventing, he soon settled down to what it is all about. We compete at riding club level and do some team chasing as well, and he looks after me very well; I don't often see a good stride, and he has learnt to sort it out for himself. I really did think in the beginning that I would never get the hang of jumping, and he scared the life out of me to start with. I hadn't jumped for years when I was given him, and Bert's idea of approaching a fence is to go sideways and keep changing legs, which is a bit off-putting if you are nervous. But once I learnt to trust him we were fine.

'Cuthbert is a very good listener, too: I give him a good ear-bashing on our hacks if I've got things on my mind – and he sometimes talks back by groaning and grumbling away as well!'

'...Tina decided that we should do the honourable thing: so they held a wedding ceremony for Cuthbert and I, and every year since Tina has sent us an anniversary card!'

Although Annie knew Cuthbert inside out from having looked after him in the yard, she had never jumped or schooled him because that had always been done by Mary. One of the funniest occasions Mary can recall is the afternoon she decided to teach Annie to jump Cuthbert. 'He wasn't the easiest horse to jump as he did get so excited,' explained Mary. 'He would jump up and down on the spot or run sideways if you tried to hold him too much. Annie was a bit unsure about jumping anyway, and the more Cuthbert tried to rush the more she held on to him, and so the more they jumped up and down on the spot, until Annie was literally bounced off him altogether! She was so upset, and she was convinced that she would never get it together with him – but once she trusted him enough just to let him go forwards they got on fine. Annie still competes and hunts Cuthbert; he has settled down a little in his old age and it is lovely to see him going across country with Annie. He is old and wise enough now to help her out if they get in a muddle, and they are a great partnership.'

Above: 'Hey!,' says Cuthbert, 'that's my carrot!'

MITSUBISHI
51

King Kong is probably best described as the joker in the pack or as Annie puts it even more succinctly, 'Conker the Plonker!' Since his arrival in Mary's yard as a cheeky but talented six-year-old his bouts of brilliance have made up for his naughtiness – he won his first two three-day events,

KING KONG

Osberton and Windsor, and was second at Burghley. However, his career has been handicapped by injury. He sustained a tendon injury whilst winning Windsor in 1992 which required a year off. Unfortunately, the injury recurred during his second visit to Burghley in 1995 and ended his three-day event career. But whatever happens he retains his zest for life, causing as much trouble in the yard as he can. But as Annie says, just as you think you really have had enough of him, one look into his big brown eyes and all his forgiven.

STABLE NOTES

PERSONAL DETAILS

16.2hh dark bay gelding, ⅞Thoroughbred

Born 1985, by the HIS stallion Newski (TB) out of Gold Imp

Stable name 'Conker'

MAIN ACHIEVEMENTS

1st Osberton 1991

1st Windsor 1992

2nd Burghley 1994

432 horse trials points

CHARACTERISTICS

Short-coupled, with very big eyes; superb jumper; very enthusiastic and rather excitable

LIKES

Competing, and outings in general; being the centre of attention; being cuddled; escaping at events

DISLIKES

Having his tail pulled – Anne is now resigned to plaiting it; teeth being rasped (has to be doped); his girth being done up tight straight away

MARY WENT TO SEE Conker as a six-year-old, when on a horse-hunting trip in Cornwall:

'I asked Hendrik Weigersma and his rider, Caroline Creighton, if they had come across any promising horses, and they put me in touch with Conker's owner, Clare Rushworth. He had been showjumping successfully as a five-year-old, and had just been turned away for a break. I was able to contact Clare's father, and persuaded him to let me come and look, even though Clare herself was out. I remember immediately falling in love with his handsome head and his twinkling, cheeky eyes – it was fairly obvious that he had plenty of character. Clare's groom was unhappy about showing him to us, as he was obviously fat and fluffy and on holiday; in fact she was just attempting to trot him up – which had resulted in Conker turning himself inside out with excitement – when Clare returned, and was promptly *furious* that we were being shown an unprepared horse. But she calmed down, and decided the best thing to do was to turn him loose in the school and let him show himself off, which he did very successfully. I was leaving for a skiing holiday the following day, so we agreed that I would come and try him on my return, by which time Clare would have put a bit of work into him.

'He was still very green on the flat, but he had a really lovely jump, balanced and neat and tidy. His trot was his worst pace; he found it very hard to keep his balance so his outline was not very consistent, and he found it hard to stay on a steady contact. But I knew all that would come with time. My only worry concerned his conformation, because he didn't have very good front limbs or feet: he was what is commonly known as "base narrow". But I liked enough about the rest of him to go ahead and buy him, subject to vet.

'The deal was that I would take Conker back to the yard so that my vet could vet him – and he failed, because of his poor conformation. I was then totally undecided about what to do, and in the end perhaps I let my heart rule my head because I finally decided he was worth the risk and that we would have him.

'As I have said, Conker was a very careful, classy jumper, but his flatwork needed a great deal of improving; in particular he found it very difficult to hold his balance in trot, and was therefore unsteady in his mouth and his head-carriage. It took quiet, consistent work on the lunge and being ridden on large circles to help him gradually to find a balance, and then he was able to hold a more consistent outline.

'He really came into his own that autumn, winning three novice events in a row...We travelled north to "do" the Scottish circuit which is always a fun, if hectic week, as you compete in three events in seven days.'

'Because his jumping was so good I was happy to start eventing him early in the spring. He had had a promising cross-country schooling session – he was a little spooky, but no more than you would expect from a careful horse – and by the end of the spring season he had picked up a few points; I remember him having one stop at his first novice, and after that he just got on with it. He really came into his own that autumn, winning three novice events in a row and his first intermediate, Auchinlech in Scotland. We had travelled north to "do" the Scottish circuit which is always a fun, if

Page 50: Going rather too steeply into the Lake at Badminton, which resulted in a stop!
Page 51: Princess Anne presents Mary and Conker with their first prize at Windsor in 1992

hectic week, as you compete in three events in seven days. His first three-day event was Osberton that September. I did wonder how he would cope with the more advanced dressage test, but he made a real effort and tried his hardest, and was rewarded by leading from start to finish. Thus by the end of his first season he was already advanced, having gained 74 points.

'As a seven-year-old the aim for him was the Windsor three-day event. He competed in a couple of open intermediate competitions early in the season, and then I entered him for his first advanced event. He had upgraded so quickly that he was still relatively inexperienced so I intended being very careful as regards not asking too much of him too soon. At Milton Keynes I felt the course asked more questions than he was ready to answer, and we withdrew after the showjumping; and I found myself doing the same at his next event; but then at Bicton I at last felt the course was right for him, and our patience was repaid with a double clear and a placing.

'Conker had one more advanced run before setting out for Windsor three-day event. Right from the start of that season I had concentrated on his obedience and discipline. He is a very good jumper but he has endless energy, and he uses this to misbehave on the flat. He had been getting very strong on one rein and I had experimented with a prickle pad, a leather cheek guard with brush bristles on it, worn on the bit against the side that the horse leans on. This encouraged him to stay straighter, and riding him in a double bridle also brought about an improvement as it made him less reliant on the hand and in a better position to begin to carry himself.

Above: Mary and Conker on the steeplechase course at Windsor in 1992 – which they won, giving Mary her fifth three-day event victory in a row

'I worked him very hard at Windsor in the lead-up to the dressage phase, with plenty of lungeing and hacking around to help settle him before I asked him to concentrate. He should have taken the lead in the dressage but for an error of course which was my fault, and which incurred a two-point penalty; this dropped us to third. On speed and endurance day he was again full of high spirits, but settled quite well on the roads and tracks phase. I remember he reared up to give himself a flying start to the steeplechase, but then settled again to the task in hand. He was superb across country, and came out on the final day to jump a lovely clear round: this won him the event.'

'He had felt rather stilted on the steeplechase and had been slightly unlevel...'

Sadly, Conker's career very nearly ended there and then. After the showjumping phase, Mary could feel just a hint of heat in a front leg. Conker was taken to the Animal Health Trust to be scanned and x-rayed, and it was found that he had a bad tendon injury. He *had* felt rather stilted on the steeplechase and had been very slightly unlevel when he finished that phase, although it had worn off quickly once he was on the roads and tracks. But obviously he had finally paid the price for his poor front-limb conformation. He was rested for the whole of the autumn and the following spring, until Dr Sue Dyson of the Animal Health Trust finally gave the all-clear to bring him back into work the summer that he was eight. She was not convinced that his leg would stand up to three-day eventing, but the idea was to see how he coped with a run of one-day events before his future was decided. He did some intermediates to get him back into the swing of things, and then ran in the advanced at Thirlestane Castle where William was competing in the final trial for the British team. He finished the autumn season with his front legs still looking in good shape, so the plan was to try him at a three-day event the following year.

'We chose Saumur because the ground is generally very good there; that was the most important factor as far as Conker's well-being was concerned. The event is early in the season so there was only

Above: 'All hands on deck!' Untacking Conker after the cross-country phase at Burghley in 1994

time for him to have two open intermediate runs and then the advanced at Dynes Hall before we travelled to Saumur, which is a three-star event. We had all our fingers crossed that the tendon would stand up to the pressure. Conker is so talented that the thought of him not having the chance to realise his full potential was too sad. He was beside himself with excitement on arrival, and I had to work him endlessly even to begin to settle him down – and in spite of all my efforts, as soon as the judge's bell rang, he just squealed with excitement. He bounced down the centre line and managed to halt just about long enough for me to salute before launching into one of the worst dressage tests of my riding career – we were lucky to stay in the arena, and managed to do very little right! Our score was so bad that there was no hope at all of pulling up into a respectable position, and this removed a great deal of the pressure and meant that I could go quite quietly round the cross-country course. Conker felt really good and jumped an excellent clear round. Uncharacteristically he had two fences down in the showjumping, but excitement was mainly to blame. The best thing by far was the fact that his tendon had held up to the rigours of a three-day event.

'He bounced down the centre line and managed to halt just about long enough for me to salute...'

'I could now plan his future with much more confidence – and the immediate future was the Burghley three-day event. I was looking forward to the challenge of a four-star event with Conker: no matter how highly you rate a horse you can never be sure whether he is genuinely a four-star prospect until you compete him at that level, so Burghley would be the chance to find out what he was really made of. Unfortunately the ground became very hard during that autumn and I was continually withdrawing Conker from events; but he did compete at Gatcombe where he finished second in the advanced class. I then missed several weeks work with him when I went out to the Hague to ride William in the World Championships, so the actual build-up to Burghley was very hectic.

'Conker had been getting somewhat above himself during my absence, and so on the way up to Burghley we stopped at Ferdi Eilberg's for some last-minute help. A belligerent Conker played up incessantly; he was getting very strong on one rein and would misbehave in an effort to evade being asked to work more evenly into each hand. Finally Ferdi got on him, and this proved to be a turning-point because Ferdi has such a strong seat and leg that he was able to keep up the pressure on Conker no matter what the horse tried to do – this meant that the leg and seat were there constantly, insisting that he listened to the aids. Finally Conker relented and gave in, and this was probably the first time in his entire life that he had fully submitted to a rider; when I got back on him the difference was wonderful to feel. Moreover the lesson stayed with him, because at Burghley he produced a lovely test which put him in second place, ahead of Star Appeal but just below William Fox-Pitt and Chaka. And on speed and endurance day he was very good indeed, willing to do as he was asked, and although a little green over some of the trickier fences, 100 per cent straight and honest. A few time penalties dropped us to third place, with Apple lying sixth. His leg was still looking in excellent shape, and just to prove how well he felt, he jumped a classy clear round on the Sunday to finish second, with Apple in fourth place.

'Dr Sue Dyson of the Animal Health Trust had been following his progress with great interest as she had predicted that his tendon would never be strong enough to stand up to a three-day event, and she was as delighted as us to have been so far proved wrong.

'The following year, in 1995, I had three horses fit, sound and qualified for Badminton, and literally right up until the night before we had to leave I could not made my mind up between Conker and Apple! I was pretty set on taking William, but the choice between the other two was very hard to

'The following year, in 1995, I had three horses fit, sound and qualified for Badminton.'

Above: Conker, Mary, William and Annie, Badminton 1995

make. At heart I was confident that Apple was a real Badminton horse because he was so bold and brave, whereas Conker, who although to date had not let me down, was that little bit more careful, and I wasn't quite sure that he would have the heart to tackle such a demanding course. But I knew that whichever horse I didn't take would have to go to Punchestown, and Punchestown is a really big, galloping track which would most definitely suit Apple. There was also the fact that Gill Robinson owned Conker, and undoubtedly she deserved the thrill of having two horses at Badminton again. These two considerations finally persuaded me to settle for Conker.

'Conker was enthralled by the atmosphere of Badminton, but tried his hardest to behave...'

'Conker was enthralled by the atmosphere of Badminton, but tried his hardest to behave throughout his dressage test, his resolve holding out until the final extended canter when he could not resist a buck and a squeal – but his mark overall kept him up in the top ten. He set off across country feeling extremely good, coping with the big fences easily and staying as straight as a die over the Vicarage Vee corner and through the Deer Park Hollow. My only real worry had been whether he would tackle the fence going into the Lake: although he had always been straight and honest, he had never given me the feeling that he was truly happy jumping into water – and the Badminton Lake is one of the biggest tests you can give a horse. I rode him very strongly at the double of rails going in, and to his credit he didn't hesitate; however, he landed quite steeply in the water which meant I had to sit right back and slip my reins completely, and I simply couldn't gather them up again quickly enough to help him get out: so he stumbled up the exit step and had no impulsion to jump the upturned punt. But he finished the rest of the course really well, and therefore proved to me that he certainly was of the calibre to compete at the very top. Our only slight concern was that he had finished very hot – even with gallons of water to wash him off, and with the fans turned on him for quite some time, it still took ages to bring his temperature down. But once he was allowed back to the stables he recovered quickly – and most important of all, his tendons were cold and hard. He had survived another big test.

'Conker had been sufficiently impressive across country for the selectors to longlist him for the Open European Championships in Pratoni in Italy that autumn. But once again the ground turned against Conker, and it was difficult to know if and when to run him. He did, however, need some preparation before the final trial which was to be at Thirlestane Castle, so I took all three horses to Shamley Green hoping for a run there; but again, the ground was like rock, and very little had been done to alleviate the problem. In desperation I took all of them just part-way round the course so at least they had done something. Since Badminton Conker had found life in general even more exciting; he obviously thought he was the big "I am' and didn't need to listen to me at all. When I trotted him to a small cross-pole to warm up for the showjumping phase he worked himself into such a state of excitement that he barely managed to take off, and became completely entangled with the poles; and amidst all the muddle I was tipped off. Normally this wouldn't have worried either myself or anyone else, but I was three months pregnant, a secret otherwise known only to Mum and Annie. Fortunately the shock of such a mistake did Conker the world of good, and he settled down and jumped a lovely clear round.

'I was beginning to realise what a worrying time Mum and Annie must have been having, knowing about my pregnancy.'

'At Gatcombe, however, the occasion got the better of him again and he was quite naughty in the dressage; and unusually for him, he also had one showjump down. I took him slowly across country. He was slightly spooky on the approach to the water, but was straight and bold at everything else. It was a day of mixed fortunes: I finished second on Apple,

but part-way round the cross-country on William, when we had a good chance of taking the lead, he overjumped a straightforward fence so extravagantly that I was jumped off – and I was beginning to realise what a worrying time Mum and Annie must have been having, knowing about my pregnancy.

'The final trial at Thirlestane Castle was now upon us, and I had to take the three longlisted horses: Apple, William and Conker. I had been able to put enough work into Conker by now to bring about an improvement in his dressage again, and this showed in a good score at the final trial. But across country he seemed to lack his normal enthusiasm, and gave me a real shock when he actually stopped at the first water complex. I know I may have been slightly too relaxed, but even without the stop he did not feel as good as usual. The selectors wasted little time in telling me that they were no longer interested in Conker, so I was free to take him to Burghley.

'Conker has always been a very enthusiastic horse, but from day one at Burghley he just did not show his usual sparkle. He didn't produce as good a dressage test as the previous year, although I was still hopeful of improving on that with a good cross-country round. But, on the steeplechase course, however, although he got round in the time, he didn't run and jump as freely as usual; yet he felt fine going back on the roads and tracks, so I put my doubts to the back of my mind. But again, out on the cross-country course I was increasingly convinced – too late – that he really wasn't quite right. He felt as though he was only jumping because I was asking him to; by half-way round he was starting to feel tired, yet I knew that he was fit and well. As we approached the Trout Hatchery I was still in two minds about whether or not to pull up – and then things seemed to happen very quickly: on the downhill slope to the water he really propped with his front legs, and seemed to have no forward power at all. He failed to take off

Above: Showjumping at Cornbury in 1995, with Conker looking happy and confident

over the fence in the water and I was thrown off, and I knew immediately that something was very wrong.

'I walked him back to the stables, and as we undid his front bandages his tendon was rapidly swelling before my eyes. The vet immediately injected him with bute [phenylbutazone] to bring down the swelling and reduce the pain, and we put ice onto both his front legs, as even his good leg was showing signs of swelling. It was *very* sad that it had to happen, although I was in a sense relieved, in that at least there was a reason for his stopping. Just sometimes, a horse competing at the highest level can simply stop enjoying it, and "throws in the towel". Conker was always so talented and enthusiastic, it would have been even sadder to think that something had happened to affect his courage. In fact the physical cause was equally as heartbreaking: Sue Dyson scanned both his legs and his weak leg showed a huge core lesion of the tendon. In her opinion the damage had started some time ago, which would have explained his poor performance at Thirlestane Castle, and the pressure of a three-day event had proved the final blow.

'...as we undid his front bandages his tendon was rapidly swelling before my eyes.'

'Poor Conker, he had been a risk from the day we bought him and he had failed the vet, and yet he had gone on to do far more than anyone might have expected; but now we were faced with the worse scenario. The only glimmer of hope was for Sue Dyson to perform a split tendon operation which, if it worked, would allow him to come back into work and compete at one-day level. He was a horse who really loved his work, and particularly his competition outings. I don't think he would be happy retired to a field somewhere, and I couldn't contemplate having him put down. He had fought back before and the operation would give him a chance to do the same again, and to continue doing what he loved.

'The operation was far quicker and simpler than I had imagined. The lower leg is cleaned and anaesthetised, and a knife is then used to cut three or four slits in the tendon. This releases all the fluid that builds up in a core lesion and which, if left, would prevent the tendon healing itself. A pressure bandage was put on which we were told to take off in thirty-six hours time. I was dreading removing the bandage, expecting to find big gaping wounds in the leg – but it all looked virtually normal; if you weren't actively looking for the signs you wouldn't have known anything was wrong. After that it was a case of pressure bandaging for an ever-decreasing amount of time, combined with controlled exercise which was gradually increased. After twelve weeks he was doing twenty minutes' walking twice a day, and both legs were looking really good. He was then sedated and turned out in a field. He will have almost a whole year out in the field, and will then be brought back into work with the hope of competing in one-day events in 1997. King Boris enjoyed several seasons of this after he was retired from three-day eventing, and Conker, who is also a great attention-seeker will, I am sure, enjoy it just as much.'

Annie on Conker

'Quite honestly Conker took a while to endear himself to me – when he came he was absolutely hopeless, wouldn't stand still for five seconds, and you couldn't leave him tied up because he would break free and go exploring. In his stable he box-walked constantly so that by the morning when you opened the door half his bed fell out into the yard and his water buckets would be completely buried! On his first day here Mary was away and so I had to take him for a hack. I found out too late that he was "cold backed" – my bottom had only just touched down in the saddle when he took off out of the yard, humping his back and tossing his head. He wouldn't let you tighten his girth properly until you were at least five minutes down the road. When he started competing he used to travel to most events with Apple [Star Appeal]. Apple was so steady and dependable that poor old Conker always appeared twice as naughty by comparison. He was a noisy traveller, always banging or tapping with his feet, and he was never very helpful about letting you put his studs in. He would start squealing with excitement as soon as he realised he was at an event, and invariably managed to escape once we arrived – and even then he wouldn't be content with just ambling off quietly to graze, but would go full tilt to wherever he could cause the most havoc! In fact he was very good about staying away at events because he always settled happily into new stabling and didn't worry about where his yard-mates were – unlike William, who would fret the whole time.

'But for all that he loved being fussed over, and a lot of his antics were really just a bid to attract attention. Underneath it all he was a very laid-back, gentle character – if he had been a person I'm sure he would love to have been a hippy in the sixties! He very quickly earned himself the title Conker the Plonker, because if there was anything within reach he would just have to investigate it; I was always rescuing things that were disappearing half-way down his throat, but he never really meant any harm. Fortunately he was very good to lead out – just like taking a dog for a walk – which was just as well, because his tendon injuries meant he was forever on controlled exercise.

'...if he had been a person he would have loved to have been a hippy in the sixties!'

'He was also very definite in his own mind about what he liked and didn't like; for example, in spite of being quite headshy he loved having his face and ears trimmed, and his muzzle rubbed – and yet he hated having his mane and tail pulled, to the point where in the end we let his tail grow and settled for plaiting it!

'Conker was a real little porker, and just loved his food; so like me and Boris, he was on a constant diet. Of all the horses he was the only one who, once he was turned out, refused to waste valuable time rolling – he left that for when he was back in his stable, usually just after you had straightened the bed out for him!

'He has only seriously blotted his copybook once with me, and I still have the scar to remind me: he spent his first long holiday in a field with two other horses about four miles from the yard. Mary was away and I was the only one working the yard at that time, so I drove over as usual to feed him in the morning. All the horses were at the gate, and I carried the three buckets of feed out and gave Conker his first. However, before I had time to feed the other two, they had rushed over to share Conker's meal. Now, Conker really likes his food and he wasn't going to share with *anyone* so he kicked out at the others, but in fact managed to hit me just above the eye. I was completely knocked out because when I woke up the horses and the food had all disappeared.

'I felt pretty sick and dizzy, but got back in the car to drive home. I hadn't realised I had been cut until I felt something wet and sticky on my face: when I took my hand away it was covered in blood! In the driver's mirror I could see I had quite a deep cut, so I drove over to Mary's mother to see if she had a plaster. Actually the first thing she wanted to do was take a photograph – telling me that I would want to see it later! – before deciding that a plaster wasn't quite enough to sort the problem out. I went to hospital and had to have stitches, and then they wanted to x-ray me as well; so in the end I got a complete day off! I couldn't get a riding hat on for a week afterwards, but other than that it was fine! And as was always the case with Conker, even when you wanted to scream at him it only took one look into his dark eyes and all was forgiven!'

Gill on Conker

'I have always adored Conker the Plonker: he is such a character. If he were a person he would be a market trader on a bargain basement stall knocking down a load of rubbish to innocent passers-by for 50p a time! He'd be unforgivably cheeky, and would *certainly* have a way with the girls! As a horse he was always a little in the shadow of King William – for example, in the year he won Windsor his success was quite eclipsed by William winning Badminton.

'My happiest memory of him was when he somehow managed to contain himself in the dressage at Burghley the year he came second. He can be so wicked, but he tried very hard to behave that day. He is the sort of character who always makes you smile because of the way he is and the things he gets up to – he can make you cross, too, but only for about half a second because with one look in his big dark eyes your resolve melts away completely.'

LAND

WILLIAM

'I was first introduced to William when he was a five-year-old: he was in a yard near Newbury and belonged to a lady called Bernice Strong, and was spotted by a friend of mine, Geoff Orrock, who had been looking out for horses on my behalf. As I drove into the yard I saw this beautiful head with a broad white blaze looking over the door and I just hoped it was him – and it was. I fell in love with him straightaway; he was such an impressive-looking horse, with tremendous presence, and he moved really well and had a good jump. It was quite late in the season when I bought him, so there was only time to take him to one novice event – which he won! Right from the start, when I rode him across country it was as though he had been doing it all his life. He would settle into a lovely rhythm and jump smoothly out of his stride, never worrying about ditches, water or banks: he was happy to jump whatever he was pointed at.'

STABLE NOTES

PERSONAL DETAILS

16.3hh bay gelding, with big distinctive blaze, $\frac{7}{8}$ Thoroughbred
Born 1983, by Nickel King out of a $\frac{1}{4}$ TB mare

MAIN ACHIEVEMENTS

Team gold European Championships 1991
1st Gatcombe British Open 1991, 1996
1st Badminton 1992
Team gold World Equestrian Games 1994
Team gold, individual bronze European Championships 1995
1,419 horse trials points
Represented GB at Barcelona and Atlanta Olympics

CHARACTERISTICS

Tall, dark and handsome; sensitive and a real gentleman; always gazing into the distance with head high

LIKES

Cross-country; dressage; having his face rubbed, or rubbing his head, usually on Annie; being clipped, trimmed and shampooed

DISLIKES

Crowds and too much applause; dressage and showjumping at Badminton!; men; staying away from home; cows; big dogs

As a six-year-old William went confidently through novice and made the transition to intermediate very easily. At this stage his dressage was not his strongest point; he was usually lying about tenth after the first phase, but he would then make up for it with good jumping rounds. He was a very impetuous horse on the flat, always wanting to rush forwards rather than waiting until his *rider* asked him to do things – it was always a case of "Hey, William! Wait for me!" At the end of his six-year-old season he went to Le Lion d'Angers to do his first three-day event: here he galloped effortlessly round the cross-country track and finished sixth, upgrading himself to advanced.

'...it was always a case of "Hey, William! Wait for me!"'

'Because he seemed to find the cross-country so easy I wasn't at all worried about his rapid rise up through the ranks. So as a seven-year-old I was quite happy to take him to Bramham which is a three-star event; to qualify for this he had to have jumped round some advanced tracks, and he did this happily. At Bramham he lay about tenth after the dressage, but after speed and endurance day he had pulled up to sixth. Moreover I had purposely not taken him particularly fast, because I wanted him to have plenty of time to see what the different problems were and to organise himself to jump them well. So it all boded well for the future, particularly as the cross-country seemed to take nothing out of him and I knew it would be easy to go up a gear and finish within the time. He showjumped clear on the last day and so held his final position of sixth.

'William's talent on the flat was starting to come through now; a great deal of quiet, steady work on simple transitions within each pace had helped him to become lighter and less reliant on my hand for support. At the three-star Blenheim event that autumn he had performed a good test and had gone fast across country to hold third place, only to lose his advantage by having three showjumps down. The going had become very muddy by the last day at Blenheim, and the showjumping was causing a lot of trouble, so I wasn't overly worried about his three fences down. In hindsight, however, this marked the start of his problems in this phase at three-day events.

William's first Badminton

'In 1991, when William was still only eight, I planned to take him to Badminton – he was just so bold across country that I didn't see any point in holding him back for another year. And my faith in him was repaid with a fabulous cross-country round; he just ate up the fences, and was desperately unlucky to be penalised for a fall on the flat. There was quite a sharp turn between two fences in Huntsman's Close, and he slipped up as he went round the corner. At that time penalty zones were still in use at three-day events: if a horse or rider fell within a certain zone marked around each fence, they were penalised as if they had fallen actually at the fence. These penalty zones have since been abandoned, and now a rider is only penalised if the fence judge considers he/she fell as a result of the way he jumped the fence. In this way a genuine slip-up on the flat is only penalised according to the time penalties incurred. For William and myself, sixty penalties for a fall knocked us some way down the placings, and he didn't help things by having three showjumps down on the last day, too. But we were all delighted with him, especially so when we were approached by the selectors: they were so impressed with his cross-country performance that they wanted to shortlist him for the European Championships to be held in Punchestown that year.'

Mishap and victory at Punchestown

'In the run-up to the Europeans, William won the British Open Championship , a title which I had won the previous year with King Boris; so we travelled out to Punchestown on a high. This was my first appearance in a British team, and I was determined to make the most of the opportunity I had waited for for so long! William performed a fabulous dressage test to take the lead on the first day; it was a performance which helped the team to a healthy lead. He then stormed round the cross-country course in fine style; I kept a good eye on my watch, too, and knew we were set to finish inside the time which would have kept us in the lead, both individually and as a team.

Page 62: Mary and William on their way to victory at Gatombe in 1996

'As we came to the penultimate fence, a big drop into water, I didn't think I needed to check him back – but the result was that he jumped far too exuberantly, and on landing his legs just buckled beneath him. I was thrown in, re-surfacing in time to see William happily jumping out the other side and apparently all set to continue to the finish, until it dawned on him that he no longer had a jockey. He pulled up rather sheepishly and was led back for me to remount. We finished without further mishap, but had obviously incurred both jumping and time penalties. Worse than that, I had wrenched my knee, and by the next morning was feeling desperately uncomfortable. Ian Stark kindly trotted William up for me at the final vets' inspection, as I myself was far too lame! – but when I tried riding him to warm him up for the showjumping I just couldn't use my leg ata all because of torn ligaments. I had to withdraw, and so our score was discarded from the team; they did, however, win the team gold.'

Winning at Badminton

'The following year, 1992, was Olympic year, and having had a taste of riding for my country I was more determined than ever to secure a place on the Olympic team. The first stage of the selection process was to ride at Badminton, and *this* time all our Christmases seemed to come at once because *William won* the 1992 Badminton Horse Trials! He had led after the dressage, and completed a foot-perfect cross-country round to remain in the lead still. As I came into the ring to showjump on the last day I knew from past experience that if he repeated his previous year's performance and had three down, then we would lose our place. He had been showjumping well at his one-day events, but the atmosphere and tension is so great at a three-day event that he never feels like the same horse. Somehow – and looking back now it seems more of a miracle than ever – William managed to lower only one pole; but such was his advantage over his nearest rival, Genny Leng and Master Craftsman, that he held on to first place – and the Mitsubishi trophy was ours. This was the first year that Mitsubishi had sponsored Badminton, taking over from long-time sponsors Whitbread. They had commissioned a new trophy, a sculpture of three horses, each depicting one of the disciplines of eventing, and one of the horses had been modelled on King William, so it was even more of a fairy tale when he won!

'Winning Badminton was such a wonderful experience: the crowd was so enthusiastic, giving William a rousing reception during his lap of honour, and then there were endless photo calls and press conferences. However, whilst I was loving every minute of the attention, we now know that William found it all very hard to cope with. He was fairly unsettled when Annie took him back to his stable, although that was to be expected after all the excitement; but in fact the atmosphere had affected him far more deeply than we realised. Once the media calls were over, Mum and Annie set off in the lorry to take him home to Devon, the plan being that David and I would follow once we had seen everybody we needed to, and generally had time to enjoy the occasion. But as we sped down the motorway later on in the pouring rain, I suddenly spotted Mum waving frantically on the hard shoulder.

'We pulled up as quickly as we could and I ran back to her, to be told that they had parked up in a service station because Annie had become increasingly worried about William – she thought he had colic. By the time I saw him he seemed quite calm, although to be on the safe side we decided I would travel back with him. And sure enough, as soon as the lorry started he became restless, snatching at his hay then dropping it, weaving and staring round wildly, and generally looking uncomfortable. We had already phoned ahead and arranged for a vet to be at the yard when we arrived, but in the meantime all I

Top: The victorious team at Punchestown (l to r) Ian Stark, Karen Dixon, Mary and Richard Walker
Above: Badminton 1992. Annie and William finally escape from the crowd's attention

between Badminton and the Olympics was relatively short; normally I would have given him about a month's holiday after an event such as Badminton, but that would not have left enough time to get him fit and ready for the Olympics which were at the end of July. However, one of the advantages of finding yourself longlisted for a British team is that suddenly all manner of expert advice is available to you from the team vet, selectors and trainers, and the general advice was that a horse

could do was to try and calm him down. Eventually I found that if I rubbed the top of his neck he seemed to relax, and that is how we spent the rest of the journey. By the time we got home and the vet saw him he seemed almost back to normal.

'In retrospect we believe that he became so wound up because of all the excitement and attention that he suffered clinical stress and colicky symptoms as a result. At the time we were too elated really to give much thought to the effect all this might have on William, but the excitement of winning Badminton and the fuss, noise and attention that went with his victory, did profoundly affect the way he behaved at future three-day events. Thus he never really settled down and relaxed at a major competition again, and certainly at Badminton we were never able to reproduce the same form in the dressage and the showjumping, only because of the tension which seemed to overtake him on arrival there. But none of this was obvious at the time, when all we could see was a bright, exciting future spearheaded by the prospect of our first Olympic Games.'

Sure enough, William was shortlisted for the Olympic team, and so a meticulous plan to prepare him for the Games was drawn up. The period of time

at rest does not start to lose muscle bulk until after seventeen days; so William had seventeen restful days in the field, after which time he was brought back into quiet work, although for the first few weeks he continued to live out in the field day and night. This change in routine in itself gives a horse a mental break from the strict routine of preparation and training during the eventing season, and for William, it made up for the fact that he could only have a short holiday.

'Now it was just a case of building up his fitness and putting some work into his dressage and showjumping so that we would produce a worthy performance at the final Olympic trial and, hopefully, at the Olympics themselves. Stephen Hadley was helping me with my showjumping, and with William it was a matter of concentrating on keeping him as soft and round in his canter as possible so that he was in a better position to use himself properly over a jump; his usual trick is to raise his head and hollow his back, and rush at his fences. Ferdi Eilberg helped us work on our dressage, advising me how to put more expression and life into William's already good paces. With a horse of William's experience you are constantly working on improving the

Above: William was first at his first event, as a five-year-old at Lulworth in 1988. He looks such a baby compared with the later pictures!

quality of his work – he knows the movements themselves inside out, so there is nothing new to teach him in that respect. Instead you work on achieving that illusive presence and expression to gain the best marks.

'I rode William in the dressage and showjumping phases of the advanced one day event at Doddington Park, and this was his only competition outing before the final trial which was at Savernake Forest. At Doddington he led the dressage and had just one showjump down, and felt very good in himself. So I went to Savernake feeling extremely confident – but our performance did not altogether live up to my expectations. William was quite tense throughout his test, and only managed second place behind Murphy Himself and Ian Stark. In the showjumping, in spite of having both Captain Mark Phillips and Stephen Hadley there to help us warm up, we still had two fences down. William did actually stay a bit softer and straighter than normal, but he was still quite onward bound and when he rushes at a fence he is not quite quick enough with his front legs to snap them up clear of it. But across country he gave me his usual Rolls Royce ride, although I did not take him particularly fast as I saw no point in risking injury at this stage.

'Fifteen horses had been longlisted for the Olympics; they all had to run in the final trial and afterwards go back to Badminton House and stable there for the night so that the team vet could carry out a veterinary inspection early the next morning. This gives the selectors the chance to see which horses look the most fit and well after the exertions of a competition, bearing in mind that at a three-day event the horses have to pass a vet's inspection after speed and endurance day, before they are allowed to showjump. William bounded past everybody the following morning looking as though he had only just come back from a holiday! We were then all left in a room to wait while the selectors had some final discussions before naming the team and reserves: a nerve-racking experience! Although I was as confident as one can be that I would be picked because of William's Badminton win, it was still a tremendous thrill and relief to hear our name called out, with Ginny Leng, Ian Stark and Richard Walker, with Karen Dixon as reserve.'

Team training at Badminton

'We had about a week at home before we were all to go into team training at Badminton House. The idea of this is to take the riders away from the distractions of their own yards at home so they can concentrate on the task in hand. It is also a time to develop a strong team spirit and generally get everyone in the right frame of mind to go out and do their best. Team members are generally given rooms above the stables and are all extremely well fed and looked after. There are photo sessions, team uniforms and riding kit to try on and try out, as well as the chance to relax with games of tennis and swimming. A special treat for me, as we do not have a television at home, is to watch videos. Some are for pure entertainment, others are meant to be part of our training and preparation!

'During team training William stayed fit and well. Ferdi Eilberg had been named as the official team trainer, although all the riders were allowed to have their own trainers to help them as well during this period. In fact I always go to Ferdi for help with my flatwork, but I was grateful for advice from Stephen Hadley and Captain Mark Phillips for my showjumping. Sadly after our last session of fastwork before we prepared to fly out to Barcelona, Master Craftsman was lame, so we lost him and Ginny from the team; but it was a wonderful opportunity for Karen Dixon and Get Smart, who stepped into her place.'

Above: Barcelona 1992, and the three-day event team relax at a party which was held for the British supporters: (l to r) Richard, Mary, Scotty and Karen

Barcelona 1992

'Before we knew it, we were in Barcelona preparing for our first Olympics. Annie and William stayed out at El Montanya, which was some way from the main Olympic village but where the stabling and cross-country course were sited. The riders moved into the Olympic village where we lived in four-bedroom apartments, each consisting of a sitting room, two bathrooms and a little kitchen – although once I spotted the food hall in the Olympic village I knew we wouldn't be using the kitchen very much! It was just amazing: there was every type of food you could think of, for every nationality, it was available twenty-four hours a day and it was all *free*! There were huge freezers full of the most wonderful ice creams, and fridges full of every type of cold drink and yoghurts. It was a food addict's heaven! One of the most exciting things about an Olympics, compared with, say, the World Equestrian Games, is that you are living and working amongst the world's best athletes from *every* type of sport. As riders this is not something we are used to, unlike track and field athletes who are meeting a wider range of sportsmen and women every time they go anywhere to compete. Event riders only ever meet event riders – so part of the excitement was to find yourself, for example, sat at the breakfast table next to Linford Christie!

'We had about a week in the Olympic village, during which time we would travel out each day to the stabling and three-day event site to exercise and school the horses. William seemed to settle in quite well, given that he finds this aspect of a competition so difficult, but he was very easily unnerved if anything unusual happened. The day before the competition started we moved down to a house just outside the stabling area so there would be less travelling for us. Also we were each allowed to school for half an hour in the big main arena where the dressage itself would be held; this was to give the horses a chance to get used to the surroundings so they wouldn't be too distracted when they came to do their test. When my turn came I was initially very pleased with the way William was working in this new environment – and then unfortunately for us, the organisers decided to test out the huge electronic scoreboard next to the arena. All William could hear was this strange rattling and whirring and he became really tight and tense, snorting and prancing and refusing point blank to go past it; even when I rode him right over to the other side he kept looking back at it as if it was going to leap out and bite him. Our allotted half hour was over before I could persuade him to settle, and I was obliged to leave with a very excited William, knowing that it would be extremely difficult now to persuade him to relax in that arena the next day.

'My dressage test was not until 6.35pm the following evening so I hoped it would be cooler and, more importantly, quieter for us by then. I rode William early in the morning, and then had a jumping lesson with Stephen Hadley when he jumped better than I have ever known him to; after that I gave him a few canters round the rotavated fast-work track to finish off his morning session. In the afternoon we had a very intensive dressage lesson with Ferdi in the course of which, although William tried very hard, he was becoming increasingly strong in my hand. By this time he had had four hours' work in all, and the plan was to leave him then, and to get on him half an hour before his dressage test.

'...part of the excitement was to find yourself sat at the breakfast table next to Linford Christie!'

'William settled down well in the practice arenas, but as soon as I headed towards the main arena he became tense and tight. Plenty of people had stayed on to watch us, and the British contingent gave him a huge cheer as he came into sight. At a big British three-day event such as Badminton the crowd usually remains very quiet until after your test, but here, the Spanish audience was very enthusiastic and continued clapping and cheering right up until the bell rang for us to start our test. Considering how tight and tense William felt he performed a very good test. I wasn't really able to ride out the movements as much as I would have liked because he was so strong in my hand, but given the circumstances he did well. By the end of the dressage phase Britain was in the lead as a team, with Ian Stark lying second, Karen third and William and I fourth. Richard Walker was further down the line, but his horse, Jacana, had performed its best-ever test – so on the whole we could not have been happier.

'I walked the cross-country course four times, and all in all felt really happy with it. I was fairly sure I would go the long way at the final water complex because it involved a very upright fence into water, and there was a good chance that William might be feeling tired by then; it is only too easy for a horse to tip up at an upright fence if he doesn't have enough energy to be quick and athletic at that stage. There was also a fence called the Owl Holes which involved jumping through a small hole in a brush fence, and the selectors had asked us all to go the long way at it as they felt the direct route was not a safe option.

'And now at last it was time to set out on the speed and endurance phase and see what we could do for our country. Richard Walker was our number one rider, and he had an unlucky refusal and fall at one of the Lake crossings; as a result of this, Karen Dixon, our number two, was told to take the long routes at several fences to ensure we then had a clear round. This she did well, but it did mean that Ian and I were going to have to produce fast clear rounds if we were to keep our gold medal position.

'On phase A, William felt great – he was covering the ground well and seemed very settled. The track was quite stony so I had to ride him carefully, and also tried to keep him in the shade as much as possible as the heat was oppressive. But then on the steeplechase I began to have serious suspicions that things could become difficult because he was becoming increasingly strong in my hand and for the first time in his life was ignoring the rubber pelham bit that he had always been ridden in. This all started as we reached the end of phase A and William spotted the crowd that had gathered to watch the steeplechase. His eyes went out on stalks, his neck shot up like a giraffe's, and it was as if he couldn't wait to gallop off, away from all these people. As there are never as many people watching the steeplechase as there are the cross-country, I knew this did not bode well for later. So although he jumped well round the steeplechase course, it was disconcerting to find that at this, the most prestigious event of our lives, I had very little control over him. However, he settled down again on phase C, and I began to feel that everything would be all right once we made our way out on the cross-country course.

'I had never experienced such a horrible feeling on a horse...William was just becoming faster and stronger.'

'In the ten-minute halt box Annie saw to William while I was briefed by the selectors about how the course was riding. I set off with the same intentions as before: to ride all but two of the direct routes. As William scorched out of the start-box he seemed unusually nervous of the spectators lining the track – in fairness they were exceptionally enthusiastic – and increasingly it felt as if he was running through my hand in an attempt to bolt away from all the people. As we neared the first of the water combinations I had to decide quickly whether or not to ride the direct route as I had originally intended. William had been jumping dangerously flat and fast, accelerating away from his fences in a bid to stop me collecting him up. The course was quite twisty, and as he refused to let me collect and balance him I was also worried about the risk of him slipping up on the flat. I just did not feel it would be safe to let him run at the water complex in this manner, and reluctantly realised I was going to have to go the long way. I had never before experienced such a horrible feeling on a horse: here we were representing our country at an Olympic Games, worse still I was in a team situation which meant my decisions not only affected me but the rest of my team-mates, and William was just becoming ever faster and stronger. In fact I ended up taking the long routes at all the water complexes, which cost us dear in terms of time penalties; and although we finished clear, I felt utterly deflated and exhausted, my gentlemanly Rolls Royce ride having turned into a complete stranger. William didn't need any attention at all at the finish, he was still bursting with energy and enthusiasm – but I felt on the point of collapse.

'Ian Stark and Murphy Himself boosted the British fortunes with a good clear, but even that was slower than Ian would have liked, the reason being

Above: Every inch a star! William and Mary at team training for the 1991 European Championships

Top: William always excites a lot of attention at the vet's inspection at Badminton
Above: William flies around the Olympic cross-country course

that the heat and humidity had taken its toll on Murphy by the last third of the course, and they could not make up as much time as they would have liked. Nevertheless, as a team we were lying second behind the New Zealanders, and as they had a team horse with a worse showjumping record than William we were quietly confident that we could overtake them and still win gold.

'Our spirits sank the next morning when Murphy Himself failed the final vets' inspection. He had hit a fence quite hard the day before, knocking an old fetlock injury, which just didn't improve enough for him to stay in the competition. So Richard's score, which included his fall, had to count, and of course this dropped us seriously down the order.

'But the next morning as I was bandaging William's legs... I was called up in front of the ground jury.'

'As our time to showjump approached I felt surprisingly relaxed. Everything seemed to point in our disfavour: I knew that showjumping was not William's strong point, on top of that I had his uncharacteristic behaviour to deal with, and having walked the course, I knew that it would not suit the less careful horses because the jumps were very bland, with little in the way of fillers to encourage the horses up in the air. Ian Stark had brought me a whole bucketful of different bits to try William in, but in the end I felt it was probably best to stick with what he knew.

'As I feared, over the practice jump William did little to encourage any optimism: he was jumping badly to the left, and just lacked concentration. When our turn came, the best I can say is that we went in and knocked five showjumps down. Richard had jumped a clear round and Karen had just one down, though we were never in sight of a medal. But as I left the arena I still couldn't help feeling pleased with William – he had gone clear across country and had finished ninth out of the world's best horses and riders. I was told off by the selectors for coming out of the ring looking happy, but I could see no point in being angry. William is not a good showjumper at a three-day event, and that is that.'

Post-Barcelona

'We came home to quite a slating from the press and public. However, you do need a bit of luck to win a major championship, and had Murphy Himself passed the vet, even with William's poor showjumping round, Ian would have had three fences in hand; and as Murphy had never had more than two down at a three-day event, our chance of gold would still have been high. We would certainly have overtaken the New Zealanders because poor Andrew Nicholson had eight showjumps down which dropped his team from gold medal position to silver, allowing the Australians finally to clinch the gold. I may be biased, but I still consider that we were unlucky; as Steve Hadley has since said, Barcelona was a case of four gold medals that got away!

'As far as William was concerned he had earned himself a holiday, his next challenge being to defend our title at the 1993 Badminton Horse Trials.'

The 1993 campaign

'Our build-up to the 1993 Badminton three-day event went well, but once we had arrived at Badminton itself it became only too obvious that William found it impossible to settle down there. Whether he remembered all the excitement and fuss of the year before, or whether he just became thoroughly over-wrought at three-day events in general, I don't know, but for a horse capable of such a good dressage test he has never since repeated his performance of 1992. In 1993 we were just in the top ten after the dressage phase. Another good cross-country performance served to lift my spirits temporarily. Not for long though, because on the last day we managed to knock down *six* showjumps, proving that Barcelona had not been just an unlucky one-off.

'A sad but adamant Bridget Parker, chairman of the selectors, came up to me afterwards to tell me politely that they would not be considering King William for a team place at the European Championships that year. Much as they admired him for his soundness and his boldness across country, they could no longer overlook his lack of showjumping prowess. I could understand their reasoning but I still considered William a good team horse, particularly when compared to the horses they had chosen in his place. But that was the end of it. They obviously felt that more work needed to be done on his showjumping, and that it had more chance of succeeding if he was not under pressure; so a team place was out of the question.

'As it turned out, the British team had a disastrous time in Achselschwang at the European Championships, with two of the team not completing the cross-country course; and so quietly I felt even more strongly about William's suitability as a team horse. My plan of campaign switched to Burghley, where I was determined to go out and show everyone what he could really do.

'But once again it was not to be. Just before his dressage test a car splashed through a ford next to where I was riding, making William jump, causing him to strike into his pastern. I cleaned the cut up, and went in to ride my test – William stayed calm and relaxed, and was the joint leader after this phase. I did ask the vet to check the wound, and he felt it would benefit from being stitched; so a neat little line of metal staples held the wound together. As William was completely sound and there was no filling at all, the vet was happy for us to go across country. But the following morning as I was bandaging William's legs ready for the big test I was called up in front of the ground jury: they simply said that as William was such a high profile horse with such a big public following they did not want to run the risk of him going across country *as it was known* that he had a small cut – rather naively I had told the press about his cut, so it had been mentioned in several newspapers.

'I was speechless! I would never dream of running a horse at an event if I thought it was in any pain or discomfort. However, my protestations were in vain, and William was withdrawn. Winning a one-day event a fortnight later I think only added to the frustration of not having been allowed to run at Burghley. Still, there was always next year.'

Badminton 1994

'1994 found us bound for Badminton once again . Although I knew this was not the ideal event for William because of the way he reacts when he gets there, it is still the event that the selectors watch for potential team members – and I was still hopeful. We had a good preparation, with William winning all three of his one-day events; but sadly Badminton was very much a repeat of the previous year: a disappointing dressage for a horse of William's calibre, a superb cross-country round, and another disaster in the showjumping, all of which left us in about sixteenth place. But the big difference this year was that the selectors were still interested in him. In spite of his unreliable showjumping they knew that his dressage and cross-country performances would always give the team a good start, and he was such a tough, sound horse that he had every chance of finishing the competition fit and well. So amid much criticism they went ahead and longlisted him for the World Championships which were to be held in The Hague, Holland, that autumn.'

World Champions

'William's autumn performances maintained the selectors' interest, and we were named as the number one rider for the team. This spot suited us well: it meant that things would probably be quieter in the dressage phase for William as he would be an early competitor, and as he is so experienced across country I was more than happy for him to be the team pathfinder on speed and endurance day. And we all accepted that what happened on the last day would be in the hands of the gods. When William performed his best dressage test to date and took the lead it began to look as if the gamble might pay off.

'The competition was not without its problems, however: the cross-country course was held in a different place to the showjumping and dressage phases, and involved a two-hour drive the night before to new stabling at the cross-country site. All the lorries from all the different countries had to travel in convoy, so it took far longer than was necessary, with the heat increasing all the time. Once in the new stabling William never really settled down; he kept pacing around, and having sweated quite heavily on the journey, continued to break out in sweat during the evening. We now know that all this time he was becoming more and more dehydrated, but because I didn't fully appreciate the import of this, I in fact set off on speed and endurance day on a horse that was not on top form. The roads and tracks phases were on deep sandy going, and in many places passed through dense woodland where the climate was very hot and humid. Although William seemed to cope well with this, it was all in fact gradually taking its toll.

'He attacked the cross-country course with his usual gusto: the first part of the course was quite twisty, and I had planned to keep as well up to speed as I could on that part but then to move up a gear on the last third of the course once we had cleared the last water. William jumped the bounce into the last water very well and cantered on through the lake to the other side. As we came to the dry ground I urged him on – and was horrified to find that nothing happened. It was as if he was still cantering through the water – he did not change pace at all, and seemed to be really struggling. My mind was in a whirl: was he ill? might he collapse? would he perhaps recover enough in a minute to pick up again? In this situation it is almost impossible to know what to do for the best and I decided to try and "nurse" him home; but if he really struggled then I determined that I would pull up. Somehow he dug deep and kept plugging on, which is eternal proof to me of his generosity. We survived the last few fences and made our way home, and as soon as I had weighed in and led William to the ten-minute box he towed me as fast as he could towards a water bucket. It was only then that we realised how dehydrated he was. The team vet stomach-tubed him with electrolytes to replace the fluids he had lost, and within minutes he was fine again. After that, all the British team horses were given electrolytes as a matter of course before starting Phase A, and none of them suffered any tiredness or dehydration.

'At the end of speed and endurance day we were lying in second place as a team; but the following morning one of the American horses failed the vet and we moved into the gold medal position. We had five showjumps in hand over the next team, and I immediately told my team-mates that they were *all* for William and me! However, they obviously didn't listen, because they used up three of them, leaving me with only two fences in hand. For most horses at this level two fences would be quite a generous margin, but we all knew that in William's case you could never have *too* many fences in hand!

'About two-thirds of the way round William took out two parts of the treble; but luckily the course then turned away from the collecting arena to a big spread which slowed him down a bit, and the next fence was quite a spooky water ditch which got him back up in the air – and then we were home! William had done it – we had won team gold – and I was just so relieved that we had not let anyone down. So the "golden girls", as we had been dubbed by the press, returned home victorious, and William lived to fight another day in the eyes of the selectors.'

Pre-Olympic Year 1995

'We found ourselves yet again at Badminton in 1995, hoping once more to impress the selectors. However, a near repeat of our previous year's performance left me less certain of a team place for the Open European Championships which were approaching that autumn. By now things were getting exciting because I was secretly pregnant – although having a horse like William to ride meant I never felt as if I was taking a risk at all. But I almost spoke too soon, because just before the final team trial we rode at Gatcombe in the British Open Championship, where a good dressage and showjumping performance meant that a customary fast clear from William would secure us victory. We were cruising along having a great round when we approached a very straightforward but big brush parallel. The next fence was away to the left, and whether William sensed that that was where we had

Above: Success at the World Equestrian Games in The Hague in 1994: (l to r) Mary, Karen, Charlotte Bathe and Kristina Gifford

to go, or whether I asked him to turn a fraction too soon I'm not sure, but whatever it was he jumped violently to the left and collided with the arm of the fence which served as an alternative. He somehow stayed on his feet but had to swerve so sharply that I went out of the side door and, complete with Emily, went rolling off down the hill! It was a very comfortable fall, but in the circumstances I thought it best not to continue.

'Things went better at the final trial at Thirlestane where William finished first, with Apple second. Sadly Apple was lame after Thirlestane, which somewhat perplexed the selectors because they had always had *him* in mind for the team rather than William – but once again William won through and found himself on the way to Italy for the Open Championships. It was a long three-day journey and we kept a very close eye on how much fluid he was getting, to be sure we had no more problems with dehydration.

'William once again excelled in the dressage, only just being pipped to the post by Lucy Thompson and Welton Romance, the eventual individual champions. I was the number one team rider again and William took Emily and me very carefully round the cross-country track, clear and inside the time, and finished very well indeed.

'Having completed our task so successfully, I felt I could at long last tell the world my secret: that I was five months' pregnant. On the last day we were once again in the lead as a team. I had three fences in hand when I entered the ring, a nice open track on grass, and William gallantly used only two of them – once

Above: William makes it all look so easy – but this photograph shows the incredible amount of strain put on the fetlock joints and front tendons

again he 'ran on' a bit through the treble which was nearest to the crowds and lowered two poles; but then he settled down and didn't fault again. Not only had we won team gold, but William had also won the individual bronze!'

Run-up to Atlanta

'Another Olympic year dawned in 1996, and because of our recent team performances where we had earned World and European team gold as well as individual bronze, I felt we had a good chance of an Olympic team place – especially as at these Olympics, for the first time, the event was actually split into separate team and individual competitions so a total of seven riders could compete, instead of the usual team of four. So I was determined to win a team place. Although the selectors now accepted that Badminton was simply not a good "showcase" for William, they could not bend the rules: if we wanted to be considered for an Olympic place we had to ride at Badminton.

'William was worse than ever in the dressage phase at Badminton, and I spoke with the selectors once again about not running him. I just know with William that I need to have a good lead after the dressage to give us some leeway on the last day, and there seemed very little point in setting off on the cross-country knowing that any advantage gained by a fast clear would be lost in the showjumping phase. But they were insistent, and so our usual fast clear followed. However, a fall at the first cross-country fence with Apple in fact prevented me from riding William in the showjumping. Although it hadn't seemed too bad at the time, my neck and back gradually stiffened up overnight and the physiotherapist who was treating me insisted that I had my neck x-rayed before I rode again.

Above: William displays his extravagant extended trot

'David whizzed me down to Frenchay hospital in the car, and according to the first set of x-rays it did indeed look as if I had fractured a vertebra. I was put in a neck brace and told not to move until I had been x-rayed again by a specialist. All the while, time was passing quickly, and William's showjumping was getting ever nearer. I rang the selectors and told them I was trapped in Frenchay; they were very supportive and told me not to rush back to ride William. They knew only too well what he could do in the showjumping phase when I was feeling my best, so one could only guess at what he might do if I was riding in pain. A further x-ray showed that nothing was in fact damaged: it had all been a false alarm. However, even a speedy drive back to Badminton was not enough to save the day, because as we arrived the last three horses were just about to jump and William had obviously been withdrawn.

'Whether or not this was for the best we will never know, but either way we found ourselves named for the Olympic squad. We had to have one last run at Hartpury College which, although it was called a final trial, was not meant to be ridden competitively. An intentionally big showjumping track was included, but William had only one down. A comfortable cross-country round earned him third place – and all too soon we were on our way to Atlanta.'

1996 Atlanta Olympics

'When we arrived in Atlanta we spent eleven days acclimatising at a farm called Pinetops, just outside the town of Thomson. For the first few days the horses were ridden quite early in the morning, before it became too hot and humid; then gradually they were worked later and later in the day so that they would be well prepared for when they had to compete in the heat. The flies were the only real problem at this stage – they were terrible, and the horses all had quite bad skin reactions which may have been either due to the flies themselves or to the amount of fly repellent we had to use. However, once we moved into the Horse Park, about 65km [40 miles] from Atlanta, this problem disappeared; the looseboxes were cool and airy, and there were no flies around at all. For the first few days the riders lived in the Olympic village, but once the three-day event began we moved down to the Horse Park. When the team and individual riders were named I was genuinely surprised to be named as an individual – although I have to confess to some relief at the knowledge that the team's fate would not be dependent on William's showjumping ability.

'Being able to watch the team competition which ran first definitely gave the individual riders an advantage in terms of seeing how the course, and in particular the terrain rode. Soon our own event was under way. I had an early draw with William which suited him well, and so far he seemed none the worse for his travels or for the strange climate. He worked in really well, and as I entered the arena I felt, for the first time in a long time, that he was going to stay really soft and relaxed. A few minutes into the test I began to realise that his performance was becoming really quite special. He was so soft and responsive, and he allowed me to ride him forwards positively through the movements. As we left the arena the crowd went truly wild – so I had not been the only one to appreciate William's performance. As the scores were read out I began to realise just how good a test we had produced: one judge had given us 191 marks, all three judges had given nines for my riding, and each judge had given us four nines for various movements within the test. William's performance turned out to be the best test ever performed at a four-star competition, and his score of 31.6 took him well in the lead. It was a fantastic feeling – I looked round and saw Annie crying her eyes out, she was so proud of "Willie". Nevertheless I knew that to succeed with William we had to have a really good lead in the dressage so as to have some room to play with on the final day; but on this occasion I could not have asked more of him.

'I looked round and saw Annie crying her eyes out, she was so proud of Willie.'

'The cross-country course was well within his ability, not overly huge or difficult, but the terrain was very awkward: it was twisty and undulating, and many of the turns had bad cambers, and we had seen the trouble this had caused in the team competition, with horses falling on the flat. Even so, I was

Behind the scenes at Badminton 1996

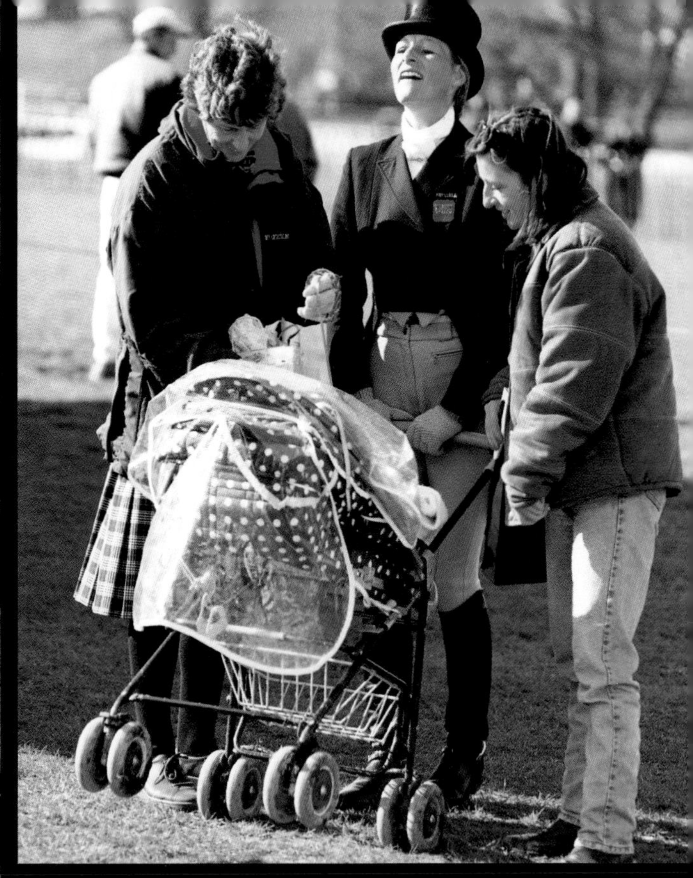

Barcelona '92
Toggi

A
A

really looking forward to the challenge. My only slight remaining worry was how William would cope with the heat and humidity after what had happened in The Hague; but I knew he was being well monitored, and as it turned out the climate was not as hostile as we had feared. The two additional stops on phase C made a tremendous difference to the horses, and William felt as bright as a button each time we set off. Also the fifteen-minute box gave us time to change his studs and for me to hear how the course was riding.

'Then we were off, and William felt very smooth and focused. Now that he is older he is not as extravagant as he used to be; he just does what he has to do. But we seemed to be keeping well up to time, and so far all appeared to be going well. Then about a third of the way round the course there was a slightly awkward dip down into some woods where we had to jump a Helsinki steps-type fence made up of log piles; this was followed by a right-hand turn to a treble of log fences – these were quite narrow, and set on a one-stride distance between. I had worried that William might jump left over the Helsinki steps, and when he did as I feared, I probably over-corrected him – and suddenly we were on a very awkward stride to the first part of the treble. We scrabbled over the first two elements but then still seemed to be too far over to the right as we reached the last element. With very little impulsion left, and faced with the guard rails rather than the fence itself, we just seemed to grind to a halt. Had he been younger I think he may still have tried to jump his way out of trouble; but being older and wiser he didn't. My heart sank to my boots, it was such a dreadful anticlimax. We had had our chance, and that was it – it was now gone. It was such a silly mistake, and needless to say, William coped easily with the rest of the course. We finished the day in 7th place, but there was little, if any hope of improving on our position, and I knew we would do well even to hold that place.

'I was keen for him to have the chance to answer his critics with another win...'

'At the final vets' inspection William was bright and cheerful, and his loyal supporters gave him a tremendous reception. There is something about William which just draws people to him – but in fact when he is standing so tall and proud whilst they applaud him he is actually terrified; he always looks as if he is lapping up the attention, but really it scares the life out of him. He was definitely nervous of that main arena. When he performed such a good test on the first day I don't think he had worked out where he was – until everyone applauded him at the end when he became very upset and uptight again. He was very tense at the final vetting, and I knew it would be the same when we went in to showjump. Chris Hunnable, our other individual rider, had gone in just before me and his horse had knocked six fences down which did not bode well for William who had a worse jumping record than Mr Bootsie.

'I knew after my telling-off in Barcelona that I had to leave the arena looking serious...'

'As William jumped the first fence my spirits rose; he made a good shape over it, and felt as if he was really thinking about what he was doing. But as we turned to the second he spotted a group of photographers, and tensed up immediately; he just ran at the fence with his head and neck high, jumping completely hollow and knocking it for six. I knew we were in for a bad time, then. I tried to support him with my hand and hold him off the fence, but then he just hollowed and took them out behind. And if I softened my hands to him, then he just ran at the fence and wasn't quick enough with his front legs to clear them. I still can't quite believe that we had eight fences down, but we did, and William dropped to thirteenth place. Any personal disappointment was nothing compared to the loss that I think the equestrian community at home felt at the complete lack of any success in the equestrian disciplines.

'I knew after my telling-off in Barcelona that I had to leave the arena looking serious and downhearted – but to be honest, I am beyond disappointment as far as William is concerned at three-day events. It was desperately embarrassing, and whilst even I never envisaged he would have quite as many faults as he did on the last day, I had always known in my heart that we would fall down the placings to some degree.'

Reputation redeemed

Once William had had a few weeks' rest in the field after the disappointment of the Atlanta Olympics, Mary couldn't help but feel that it seemed a very long time until the start of the next season. He looked extremely well in himself, and was alert and interested in all that the other horses were doing, so she decided to bring him back into work for the last few events of the season. she particularly wanted him to have the chance to run in the Open Championships at Gatcombe Horse Trials; he has always relished the cross-country course, and having won the title twice before, Mary was keen for him to have the chance to answer his critics with another win there.

'I knew some people might be critical of my decision, because it is traditional for horses to finish their season after their autumn three-day event. But the Olympics were held much earlier than the usual autumn three-days, and as it turned out, I wasn't the only Olympic rider with this idea in mind. To be on the safe side I rang Bridget Parker, the chairman of the selectors, to see how they viewed my decision, and the general feeling was that if the horse looked fit and well, then to go ahead. Certainly William had lost very little fitness, and it didn't take much work to pick him up again and prepare him for Gatcombe.

'Although I felt happy in my own mind about taking him, I was quietly relieved to see that a number of other riders had entered their Olympic horses. He produced a good dressage test – not quite up to his Atlanta standard, but good enough to take the lead. And the following morning he showjumped well, with just one showjump down in what was a big track; in fact he jumped as well as he normally does at a one-day event, which was a relief after our disastrous round in Atlanta. This dropped us into third place behind my other ride, King Solomon. Solly had been third after the dressage, but had showjumped clear to move up into second place.

'Plenty of people made sure they were around to watch William showjump, and although I of course always long for him to jump well, I no longer worry about it. As far as I'm concerned, once we are in the showjumping arena, what will be, will be, and I feel neither nervous nor disappointed. I have tried everything I can, and I now accept that some days it will go well, and other days it won't. However, it was nonetheless most gratifying that he redeemed himself in the eyes of those who still ove him!

'We set off on the cross-country, and William reminded me yet again just what a dream he is on this phase. He knows the course here well, now, and gave me a fantastic, smooth round; he felt comfortably within himself, and recorded a good time. The cross-country phase is run in reverse order of merit, but because I also had Solomon to ride, I had gone earlier than normal on William. So it was quite a wait before I knew whether he had done enough to claim victory. And he had: he had won his second Open Championship title, and had given his fans good cause to be proud of him.

'Having seen how much he enjoyed his outing I decided to keep him in work for a few more weeks and let him run in the special advanced section at Lulworth horse trials. This was Willie's final outing of the season, and with £1,000 prize money on offer, this was always going to be a very competitive section! He produced a most pleasing test to gain a score of 23, although it was still only good enough for second place. The showjumping phase had been made slightly more complicated by the innovative idea of allowing riders to choose their own line – in other words, the most direct route around the course consisted of several tight angles and turns, or you could go the longer way round which would almost certainly incur time faults. William had just the one fence down, but he did also incur two time faults; this was partly because I knew that if I let him gain too much speed he would have more fences down, so although we took the quickest routes, I had to keep him in a very short, bouncy canter.

'The cross-country was run in reverse order, and by this time we were lying in fourth place. I went round at what I felt was a fairly fast speed, holding tight lines and wasting no time at all, and picked up thirteen time faults which I thought would be good enough to move us up a place or two. But with so much prize money on offer, and with it being almost the end of the season, most of those within a shout of the prize money flew round very fast, pushing us back to fifth place. Nevertheless, it was still a very happy event to end the season with, and William felt as if he had enjoyed every minute of it.'

William's Future

'I know now that William's major championships career is over. His tenseness is nothing more than the stress of nerves, because he jumps beautifully at home; but he obviously cannot take the pressure of the final phase of a three-day event. To me he is still the most fabulous horse, and no one can take away his victories, which have been many: he is now the second highest points-winning horse there has ever been in the sport of eventing.

'His future career is going to be planned for fun. I will ride him at one-day events, and if he ever does another three-day event it will be somewhere less prestigious and pressurised than Badminton.'

Annie on William

'When William arrived in the yard, my first reaction was that he was the most beautiful horse I had ever seen. My second thought, as he stood at the top of the ramp with his head high in the air, was "Oh not another enormous one!" Initially he was a big baby, and found all sorts of things quite scary until he settled into the routine of the yard, but then he seemed to gain confidence from that. He was particularly terrified of cows, and if they came anywhere near him on a hack he would gallop off; and he still is a bit difficult with heavy traffic. If he is being led, however, he puts his faith entirely in the other horse and is as good as gold.

'It may sound silly, but William has undoubtedly opened up my world: if it were not for him, I would never have been to so many wonderful places – the Olympics, the World and European championships as well as Badminton, Burghley, Gatcombe and Punchestown. He is quite a complex character, sometimes very aloof and ignoring me completely, at others really seeming to need a person to be there with him to help him feel secure. He appears to draw a great deal of confidence from other horses; for example, if he stables overnight at an event he immediately falls in love with the horse next to him, and becomes extremely agitated if his neighbour is taken away. So he is quite difficult to manage at three-day events, because you always have to be keeping an eye on him in case he has suddenly found himself on his own and is working himself into a state. If anything is wrong in his little world he gets very upset. But at home in the yard he is a gentleman to deal with; angelic to clip and trim, and really enjoying the attention, evidently finding it all very relaxing.

'William is the sort of horse which is at its best when kept in a consistent routine; he loves being turned out, for instance, and obviously looks forward to that part of the day – generally he is probably happier out of his stable than in it. Now that he is getting older he likes to be ridden out in the second session of the morning so that he can have his breakfast and then go back to sleep for an hour. He is very quiet in his stable, usually happy just to stand still with his head out of the barn window watching the world go by; that is how I always picture him.'

Annie's Barcelona

'The Barcelona Olympics in 1992 were obviously a tremendous experience. The whole build-up to our going was so exciting, although it only really sank in once we were in team training and had collected all our Olympic kit. I had never imagined that we would be given so many things: British Olympic shorts, tee-shirts, sweatshirts, tracksuits, training shoes, watches, suitcases and hat covers – it was just unreal, and on top of all that there was the equipment provided by the official team sponsors, such as rugs and boots for the horses, grooming equipment and so on. It was just like several Christmases coming all at once!

'In fact I was quite anxious about the prospect of William having to fly out there: I had flown with horses once before, and the whole procedure had worried me considerably. However, I need not have feared, because the team that was responsible for flying us to Barcelona were true professionals. During team training everyone had been joking about not wanting their horse to be next to William on the flight because it was generally considered that *he* would be the one to get really wound up; so his flying companion was a very experienced Portuguese dressage horse, and it did indeed have a wonderfully calming effect on him. We had been told to make sure the horses were quite hungry before the flight so that they would be content to settle down and eat once they were en route, and loading up was easy because

Left: All dressed up for the photographers at team training at Badminton

the transit crate is built round the horse so it doesn't have to walk into an enclosed space. And indeed, Willie settled down perfectly happily, and munched his haynet and enjoyed the air-conditioned ride.

'The only real problem came when we landed in Barcelona and found that the airport did not have a ramp to lead the horses down off the plane. They set about making an alarmingly shaky construction out of plywood, and I wasn't at all happy about taking a horse down it – but couldn't really see what choice we had. Willie had to go first, and as soon as his feet touched it he set off down it at a canter. I was being dragged along next to him and could envisage us both landing in a mangled heap on the tarmac, but luckily one of the officials was brave enough to stand at the end of the ramp and wave his arms at Willie to back him down, so we landed just about in control.

'The stables we had been given were very small, but at least Willie's was in the shade; we rigged up a fan in the doorway, too, and he soon learnt to come and stand by it to cool off.

'Once we had arrived, the procedure was the same as for any other three-day event, although the heat made it more tiring. It didn't seem to affect William, however, who shocked Mary by pulling like a train and forgetting all his usual manners – at the final trot-up he looked the fittest and happiest horse there. Another unusual arrangement was that the showjumping was held on a different site to the dressage and cross-country, so to try the already taut nerves on the final day we had to transport the horses down into Barcelona to the big stadium. William's costly showjumping round has been well reported and criticised time after time – yet we knew that he had done his best. The fact that he becomes tense in the showjumping is a part of his character, and not because he is ungenuine or careless; in the same way that a human athlete cannot perform well if his body is tense, nor can William. So we were still very proud of him, and just relieved that he had survived his first Olympics so well and was, at the end of the day, still amongst the top ten horses in the world.

'The journey back to the stables was not without incident: it should have taken about forty-five minutes, but the police escort must have thought we were heading straight back to England because it escorted the horse transporter all the way to the Spanish border before conceding that this was not the planned route and eventually taking us back to the stables. As a result, the journey took three very long hours! We stayed in Barcelona for another week so that our horses could fly back with the showjumpers. That week was brilliant: William's routine was to be ridden bareback by me in my bikini, up to the steeplechase course where there was lots of lush grass. He would munch away while I sunbathed or read a book, then I would take him back down to the stables where he would enjoy a cool shower before having his afternoon siesta.'

The Hague, 1994

'Having coped with Barcelona, I really considered that anything else we might ever have to do would be a doddle – but how wrong I was, because the World Championships held in The Hague were reminiscent of a survival camp. The biggest advantage was that we travelled there in our own lorry, with Mary and I sharing the driving, so we knew that part of the excursion should be all right. But when we arrived we found the stables were far too small; so in true British spirit we knocked two stables into one for William. This meant I lost the area that had been designated to me as a tack room, so all our equipment had to be kept outside the stable. There wasn't enough room to tie a horse up outside the stable, either; it seems the organisers of stabling at so many big events fail to appreciate how much room you need to work round a horse, and there are

Above: Cramped conditions behind the scenes at the Barcelona Olympics

a great many jobs which are more convenient to do outside, such as grooming, cleaning out stud holes and washing off.

'Despite all this William seemed very settled, and for him, almost laid back. He remained relaxed in his dressage test, too, even though they were still building the stadium around him when he got there. It was one of the best tests that I have seen him do, the other being the one he performed at Gatcombe when he won the British Open Championship for the first time: the test at Gatcombe was that of a lovely young advanced horse trying its hardest to perform the movements; at the Hague it was that of an experienced advanced horse which knew only too well how to do the movements as long as he could keep himself relaxed enough to perform them impressively.

'Looking back, we now know that in The Hague he was gradually becoming dehydrated because of the hot, humid climate, a condition which deteriorated dramatically on speed and endurance day when he really struggled over the last few fences on the course. It was truly alarming to see William in such a state, because as a rule he always made the cross-country phase look so easy. Luckily he recovered quickly: John Killingbeck, the team vet, immediately drenched him with fluids which countered the effects of dehydration, and within half an hour he was back to normal. We learned from that how important it is constantly to monitor the horse's water intake and to look for signs of dehydration, the most obvious being that the skin remains pinched up if you squeeze it between your fingers; normally it would flop back smooth and flat into place.

'At all his three-day events William has proved to be a very tough, sound horse. There are never any panics the night after the cross-country as to whether or not he will be sound for the final inspection, and in that respect he is a pleasure to manage. With Conker, on the other hand, we always had to be ready to apply as much cold as we could to his legs, in the form of ice packs or cold hosing, after the cross-country to help ensure he was fit and well for the final vetting.

'Over the years the showjumping has become the most fraught phase of any three-day event with William. He seems to be able to forget his tensions and worries on the speed and endurance, but they all come back to haunt him on the last day when he becomes very tense and insecure; and as I said earlier, it is the physical tension in his body which makes it hard for him to use himself athletically over a showjump. But even though we know that what he does in that phase is really in the hands of the Gods, it is still hard not to allow your hopes to be raised, especially as he is nearly always in a strong position after the cross-country.

'It was therefore common knowledge amongst the British team in The Hague that William's showjumping might be the weak link on the last day. Because he was the highest placed of the team after the cross-country, he was the last of them to showjump; so for William it was important that the others jumped clear, giving him that vital headway so that he could afford to make a mistake or two. But as each rider went in, it became clear that he was going to have to jump well if we were to keep team gold. Karen Dixon and Charlotte Bathe had both had fences down, and this had narrowed the winning margin so the pressure was building all the time.

'William was lying in third place individually, and Mary was just so cool about it all! She only got on him about five horses before his turn; after going through a few of the flatwork exercise that Lars Sederholm had given her, she then jumped a couple of warm-up fences – and I was horrified when William completely flattened the practice fence, wings and all! Stephen Hadley, the team trainer, seemed to have vanished but luckily David Broome saw what happened and came over to help me rebuild it. He was so calm; he had never helped Mary before, but he just said "Come in slowly, Mary, and give him as much room as possible" – and William cleared it well. Then it was time for her to go in; Lars had suggested that she ride William in on a long rein and let him have a good look at everything – before, she has always held him up together in an effort to keep his attention on the jumps and not on the crowds. So it was really weird to see this new approach being tried for the first time, and I didn't know whether to laugh or cry as William entered the arena gazing around at his surroundings like a giraffe. But it seemed to work; he made a couple of mistakes, but it was a good enough round to keep the team gold medal. I was just so proud of them both!'

Keeping the big secret

'I think I probably felt happiest for William at the Open European Championships in 1995 in Pratoni, Italy, because here, at long last, not only did William help win the team gold, but he also won his very own bronze medal. Once again I was worried about him on the journey down: he started to lose weight, but luckily we had the team vet travelling with us, and he kept drenching him with fluids so that when we arrived William was in excellent condition and spirits. Yet again the stabling area was cramped, but William is very careful in his stable, always looking before he rolls or lies down so he is unlikely to cast himself. Nevertheless, the conditions generally were far better, and both the course and the setting were fantastic. Being led out to graze for an hour each day helped to keep both William and myself relaxed – he ate while I read – but the biggest relief of all was that Mary had at long last announced publicly that she was expecting a baby; so I could really relax, as I no longer had this awesome secret to keep.'

In 1995 Mary surprised even her closest fans by announcing, on the day she won an individual bronze medal and team gold at the Open European Championships, that she was five months pregnant. It didn't need a long memory to realise she had survived falls at Gatcombe and Burghley a month earlier, and yet had still ridden with immaculate trust and confidence round the big championship course in Italy. Having safely given birth to Emily Maria in January 1996 she was back on King William at Badminton just three months later. After a successful clear cross-country round, watched by young Emily dressed in her mother's cross-country colours, it was no surprise to hear Mary announce during her press interviews that 'William is my best friend'. Whilst William obviously had no trouble keeping quiet about Mary's secret, Annie found it very difficult indeed – although to her eternal credit, she succeeded. As she recalls:

'When Mary came back from her honeymoon, I went off for my own summer holiday. A few days after I returned I was out hacking with Mary when she suddenly said, "I've something really exciting I just have to tell you", and I knew immediately what she was going to say, and I was so pleased for her. I am the youngest in my family, and have experienced all the anticipation, the excitement and the happiness involved when my sisters were pregnant; so when she told me I had to keep it a secret I knew it would be difficult. The only person I really desperately wanted to tell was my mother, because she follows always everything that we do in the yard so enthusiastically; but I knew that if I told one person then I wouldn't be able to stop! I felt it was Mary's choice, and although there was obviously some risk involved, she is an excellent rider, she has a good team of horses, and above all, she would limit the risks she allowed herself to take. Her husband David, her mother and her doctor all knew, and she had their backing.

'The fact of her pregnancy didn't seem to make very much difference to anything we did; I know the heat affected her quite badly, and I suppose I was very aware not only of looking after the horses, but also of making sure that Mary wasn't doing too much, and that she was eating enough! I always breathed an extra sigh of relief when she finished a cross-country course; the couple of falls she had that autumn were worrying in that you couldn't voice your greatest worry straightaway, in public, but had to wait until you were on your own again.

'Now that Emily has arrived, things are very much the same as they were in the yard – thanks really to Mary's mother who looks after her for so much of the time. I perhaps don't see Mary for as long in the afternoons now, but I can generally reach her by phone. She always used to do the evening feeds because it gave her a chance to see each of the horses quietly, on its own, but now Mary's mum will quite often come in to do that, having played "grandma" to Emily in the morning. I don't know what any of us would do without her; because she lives just down the lane from the horses she will always pop back and look at any horse that needs checking over after we have gone home. On top of that she keeps us stocked up with food when we are travelling to events, and will even do my shopping for me during the week, as well as help with any heavy work we are doing in the yard – and that includes concreting and bricklaying! I am sure it is this "family effort" which has helped to keep such a happy, relaxed atmosphere in the yard, something that the humans benefit from just as much as the horses.'

Opposite top: Phase C, the first cooling stop. Before the event the riders and horses were given a chance to get used to the fans and misting machines

Annie in Atlanta

'Team training at Badminton seemed more hectic than usual this time. There was all the usual packing and organising of equipment, but I think taking Lillie [King's Mistress] into training alongside William made for a great deal of extra work. She fell head over heels in love with William and became quite naughty every time he left the yard. With that, and her habit of playing football with her water buckets at night, I was kept busy keeping her in order. William was good and steady the whole way through; he seems to know the difference between Badminton when it is a competition and when he is there for team training.

'On the Sunday, Lillie was taken back down to Devon by Mary, and I was left with William. Our journey to Stansted airport started after lunch, and all the way there I could feel the excitement really building up. At the airport everything was extremely well organised; even though we had not been told that the flight had been brought forward an hour, so in theory we arrived an hour late, the airport people handled it all very well, and in the end it just meant less hanging around when we got there.

'Only four of the team grooms could travel in the plane – the horses are loaded into crates in pairs, and one groom travels with that pair of horses. Some of my friends had already flown out ahead of us. William was travelling with Charlie [Charlotte Bathe's horse, The Cool Customer] and I was looking after the pair of them. The horses are walked into their travelling crates, which are then picked up by a forklift truck and loaded into the plane. This part of the proceedings is probably the most unsettling for them. Once they are in the plane they just settle down the same as if they were in the lorry. They had all had their food cut back the day before so that they would be hungry once they were loaded, and sure enough they were all happy to tuck into their hay and relax. My only worry during the flight was that both Charlie and William refused to drink anything, but I told our vet, John Killingbeck, and once we had landed and they were stabled he stomach-tubed them with fluids to prevent any risk of dehydration.

Centre: William making full use of the lunge ring, something he did once a day, if not twice!
Above: One very wet afternoon William's stable was a wash out!

'It was an eight-hour flight, and we landed at about four in the morning. We then had to put the horses in quarantine for forty-eight hours, which was a new experience for me. All their clothing, such as summer sheets, bandages and travel boots, were taken away and washed, and the horses themselves were then examined from top to toe – I think the quarantine officials were looking for things such as ticks and other parasites. The horses were then given a wash all over with a vinegary solution before being allowed in their stables, and their heart and respiration rates and temperature were monitored continually. The rules in quarantine were very strict – we were only allowed in for certain hours each day, and the rest of the time the resident staff saw to the horses. When we did go in we had to wear paper suits and slippers; William was terrified of me in a paper suit, which made grooming and walking him out quite difficult! The horses were not allowed outside at all: we could walk them round the big hangar that we were in, but that was it. But the air conditioned stables were really good. When we had landed at the airport the heat had hit you like a wall, so we were probably in one of the best places.

'After the quarantine period we headed out to Pinetops, the farm where we were all based to acclimatise. We travelled out in big horse transporters, and William didn't enjoy the journey at all – he was on the traffic side of the lorry, and the noise and rush of the traffic passing him obviously upset him. I was very glad when we arrived and could get him off and into a stable. The stabling was large and airy, and each box had its own cooling fan, but flies were a real problem. The grooms all stayed in a little wooden house next to the yard – we called it the Waltons because it reminded us all of the house in the television series. Mary flew in the day that we arrived there and seemed very pleased with how William looked, so that was a relief. From a work point of view it was then all quite relaxed. The horses were not allowed to do too much to begin with, and it was done early in the morning; so the rest of the day was spent trying to keep them comfortable because of the flies, leading them out to roll in the sand-pits which William had come to love, and generally making sure we had all the tack and equipment up together, ready for the actual competition.

'After a few days we found that William was

Above: Late morning after William had exercised and grazed. The two trunks had to hold *all* the equipment including saddles, rugs and even Mary's riding gear!

getting rubs on his legs from his Woof boots. All the horses were coming up in various little lumps, bumps and sores because of the heat and the flies, so we rode him in bandages after that. We did have another scare when his girth area became swollen – again I think this was because the horses were sweating so much more than usual – so we had to put a soft sleeve on his girth, something he has never had to have before.

'William stayed very relaxed and settled in himself; all the horses had been trained almost to peak fitness at home, because we knew they would have to take things quietly on arrival until they acclimatised, so I think he thought he was on holiday. He would go out for a quiet hack, then be led out to graze and have a roll, before going back to his box for a sleep in the afternoon! I also started to give him a late night feed, which he thought was great. We never do this at home, but everyone else gave an extra feed at night and I thought it was unfair on him if he had to stand and watch them all munching away, so he joined in the new routine. His work was picked up gradually until he was doing a little bit of cantering and jumping. Then we all moved down to the Olympic Horse Park at Conyers. We made sure William was on the quiet side of the horse transporter this time, and he travelled quite happily.

'The stabling and facilities in the Horse Park were even better, and there were hardly any flies which was an enormous relief. We moved into little mobile homes, each shared with three other people. There was a huge laundry with hundreds of washers and driers – the only slightly disappointing thing was the food, which was designed more for convenience than for taste. From the groom's point of view the organisers had thought of just about everything: there were ample washing-down areas, water pipes and taps in convenient places, several lungeing rings – which William used for rolling in – and plenty of arenas for riding in, as well as good all-weather galloping tracks. The only thing we lacked was a bar or some central venue for socialising in the evenings – there was no real meeting place in that respect, so our team farrier used to collect us in a minibus and take us to the hotel where our vet, John Killingbeck, was staying, and that became our social centre!

'I clipped William just a few days before the competition began; I used fine blades and was surprised at how much coat came off, so I was glad I did it. Just a few days before the first official horse inspection we were told that William and Mary would run as individuals. I was quite shocked at first because I think we had all considered Willie to be very much a team horse – but the more I thought about it, the happier I was with the decision. My personal worry all along was whether William would cope with the heat and humidity, and as an individual it would be far easier for Mary to make the decision to pull up if she thought he was struggling. So from our own point of view I then felt much happier about the whole competition.

'As far as our event was concerned, there seemed to be such a long wait before it was our turn to go. And it was strange to watch the team through almost the whole of their three-day competition before we even started the dressage phase of ours. There was a veterinary inspection for all the horses, team and individual, two days before the team event started, and then we had another trot-up the day before the individual competition began, so in that respect, too, it was all quite strange and drawn out.'

Olympic Competition

'Our dressage day was very busy because it was the same day as the team cross-country event. So in the morning I was helping where I could in the fifteen-minute box, but then had to rush back to get William ready for his dressage. I had plaited him up early in the morning so that Mary could work him for as long as she wanted to later in the day in case he took a long time to settle down. She hacked him out in the morning and worked him again in the afternoon, coming back much sooner than I had expected to report that he was beautifully relaxed and had probably done enough. She rode him for about half an hour before his test, and then off they went – to give the performance of a lifetime! We all went out that night and celebrated.

'The next day Mary gave him a jump in the morning and then took him for a hack. In the afternoon I walked the course – I thought it was pretty big and very twisty, and although I felt it was well within William's ability, I wasn't so sure about the slippery terrain.

'On cross-country day I was up at 4.30am to feed William. Mary didn't want him plaited, so there wasn't too much else to do. I always leave the front bandages for Mary to put on, and in that last hour before they set off we keep everything pretty quiet. We all know each other inside out now, and just get on with our jobs and wait for the countdown.

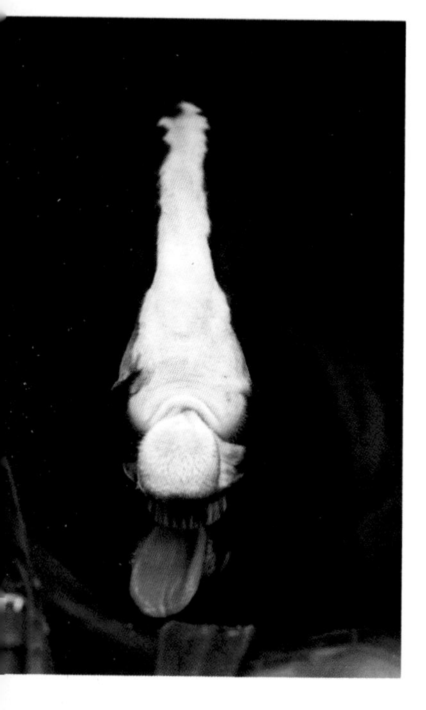

'Mary set off on phase A at 7.30 in the morning. Straightaway I had a panic because I couldn't find a shuttle to take me back to the steeplechase track – there was meant to be one every five minutes, but after ten minutes I decided I couldn't wait any longer and set off on foot; luckily someone stopped and gave me a lift. William looked very good indeed on the steeplechase; then I had to hurry ahead to get to the first of the compulsory cooling stops on phase C. Usually there is plenty of time to get back from the steeplechase to the ten-minute box, but because of the two cooling stops which had been incorporated in phase C it all seemed a real rush; I had only just got things organised in the box when Mary and William came trotting in. The extra stops had certainly refreshed William and he was looking extremely good. We needed the full fifteen minutes in the box as Mary wanted all William's eight studs changed to much bigger ones because so many horses still seemed to be slipping on the flat. And then they were away again.

'I wasn't quite sure where to go at this point, because I really wanted to see as much as possible. However, I could make out a monitor through the commentator's box, and watched from there. When William stopped I just felt completely numb. My first thoughts were how disappointed Mary was going to be, and the rest was just a feeling of complete anticlimax. We were not going to win a medal. But then you

Above: William gives his opinion on the photographer!

Above: The vet's inspection in the sizzling heat of the Atlanta Olympics

put all these feelings behind you, and all you want to see next is your horse and rider back in one piece.

'William's heart and respiration rates were still good when he finished. We had to keep the horses there for half an hour after they had finished so there would be plenty of help on hand if a horse did suddenly start to feel the effects of what he had just done. But as soon as we were allowed to go I took William back down to the stables. He had pulled both his front shoes loose, so I put Icetight on his legs and bags of ice around his feet. The farrier came later in the day and tightened up his shoes and then I put another poultice on each foot just to be on the safe side. I washed his legs off that evening and he had only stable bandages on overnight; his cross-country had all been over by 9.30am so he had already had Icetight poultices on for twelve hours, and there was no need to leave them on overnight.

'As far as I am concerned, William is the greatest...'

'The next day Mary came down early to ride him out before the final trot-up. He looked and felt really good, and put on his usual performance at the horse inspection. All the horses looked fit and well at the inspection – so often many of them are stiff and tired, but from a welfare point of view this event was a complete success.

'On showjumping morning we worked William quietly in one of the arenas, just going through the usual warm-up exercises that we would do at home, trotting to fences and then cantering to them, with Mary concentrating on keeping him as relaxed as possible. But as he entered the arena you could see him change completely – he became tense and worried, and I knew immediately that we couldn't expect a good result. When I realised just how bad his performance *had* been, I felt awful both for Mary who put so much work into trying to improve this phase, and for William who seems quite unable to help himself on the last day of a three-day event. *We* all know he can jump beautifully, and that is what makes it so heartbreaking – but no one can tell him there is nothing to worry about on the day that really matters. People very quickly forget just how much he has done: he has won team World and European gold medals, an individual bronze, as well as Badminton and Gatcombe. After his previous two team performances it really did look as if he was learning to cope – but sadly it wasn't so. The worst aspect of it all was coming back home and having to tell people all over again what went wrong.

'William travelled home the next day, oblivious to the disappointment of the British camp. I thought it would all prove a bit stressful for him, having to turn round and fly home so quickly, but he travelled better than he has ever done and actually put on weight during the journey. Mary's mum and my best friend Tina came to meet us and took us back to Devon. William got so excited once he realised he was nearly home – he was whinnying frantically and tore out of the lorry to see his buddies. No one could believe how fit and well he looked and even he didn't seem to want his holiday to begin.

'As far as I am concerned, William is the greatest, and in spite of everything that has and will be said about his performance, no one will ever convince me that he is anything other than a champion.'

Annie at Gatcombe

'After William's fabulous dressage test in Atlanta, it is very easy to expect him to reproduce that sort of standard every time now; his test at Gatcombe, however, wasn't quite as good – although it was still excellent considering he had been on holiday only a few weeks before. He also managed to contain his nerves: he knows Gatcombe as well as Badminton now, and last year his test had been slightly spoilt by his over-excitement; but this time he worked really well.

'When he went in to showjump, although Mary says she doesn't worry about what he does in this phase any more, I was still a nervous wreck! He hit the first fence really hard and I just wanted her to pull up and bring him out of the ring – so it's just as well she didn't! But after that mistake you could see William really trying, his legs seeming to go in all directions in an effort not to hit anything; and bless him, he managed to clear the rest.

'On the cross-country my only worry was whether he was really fit enough, but I needn't have worried – it was soon obvious that he was just loving every minute of it. He is still such a popular horse, even though for the really big occasions he still sorely tried everybody's devotion to him; so it was quite an emotional feeling when, after all the upsets of Atlanta, he came out and gave everyone something to be proud of again.

'In spite of the disappointment not only of William's overall performance, but the British team's as a whole, I thoroughly enjoyed my Atlanta experience: it was fantastic for me to get to another Olympics, and even more special as it was with the same horse and rider. I really enjoy being part of a team, and sharing in the feeling that you are representing your country. The Horse Park at the Atlanta Olympics felt very much more a part of the proceedings than the one at Barcelona. In Spain we were stuck up in the mountains and it was just like being at another three-day event - there was very little to remind you that it *was* an Olympics. But the Horse Park for Atlanta had much more buzz. The facilities were superb, but what really made the Games for me was being allowed to go to the opening ceremony. We marched into the stadium with all the other athletes, and it was just unreal! American razzamatazz is quite something to experience.'

Gill on William

'There is no doubt that, if he were a person, William would be the ultimate film star: tall, dark and handsome, a bit of a Gregory Peck, constantly fighting off the women! He would also be an absolute gentleman, always bringing you flowers and chocolates. I knew he had star quality the first time I saw him: Mary was riding him at a novice horse trials so she was wearing only her hacking jacket and riding hat, but all I could picture was William in the dressage arena at Badminton with Mary in her top hat and tails. On that very day I told Mary that William would win Badminton!

'William has been the horse of a lifetime, and I do feel proud and privileged to have been a part of his team. What I really love is the pleasure he brings to so many – you only have to see how the crowds follow him, particularly at occasions such as the trot-up at Badminton, to realise just how much people love and admire him. In 1992, the year he won Badminton, Hugh Thomas had asked Mary if she would have time to see a young autistic man who was very keen to meet her. I suggested he met William as well, but Hugh was a bit nervous about how a highly strung, fit Thoroughbred might behave. But we had no doubts about it, and the young man met Mary and William straight after they had completed their dressage test. The crowds were ecstatic because he had performed such a beautiful test and hundreds of people were milling around him. But when the young man came forwards William gently lowered his head and stood as quietly as could be while he stroked him. For me, that proves what a very special person William is.

'But when the young man came forwards William gently lowered his head and stood as quietly as could be while he stroked him...that proves what a very special person William is."

'William has brought me so much pleasure in so many different ways that it is difficult to pick a favourite memory. Obviously the win at Badminton was fantastic, but I think I am equally proud of his achievements in winning Gatcombe in 1991, the year after King Boris had won it with Mary; and his performance at the World Championships in the Hague again served to emphasise what a brave, genuine horse he is.

'As the owner, rather than the rider of the King string, my view of the horses is often quite different to that of Mary or Annie. Although I do visit the yard fairly frequently, I generally see the horses at their "parties" rather than in their day-to-day training routine. Usually everything goes well, and I compare it to the impression you get of someone if you only ever meet them at posh occasions when they are obviously on their best behaviour! You don't actually see the darker side of their nature unless they have one too many to drink and their cover slips a little. So when things go wrong at an event it is quite an eye-opener for me: the polite cover has slipped and I am seeing another side to their character!'

In the past, most of Mary's horses were bought either by herself and husband David, or by Gill Robinson; more recently sponsorship has played a vital role in the running of the team. Star Appeal, however, was bought for Mary to ride by the Pinder family, for whom

STAR APPEAL

she had previously ridden: 'When I left Sheila Willcox's yard I had the summer free before going off to do my year's cooking and as chalet girl. I bought a five-year-old, put a great deal of time and effort into producing it well, and sold it to the Pinders. They kept in touch with me, and at about the time that I had Diver's Rock, they asked me to compete another horse they already owned, a grey called Silverstone. They seemed to enjoy the eventing scene and all the ups and downs of being an "owner" very much, and this culminated in their asking me to look out for a promising type of young horse which they would buy and I would produce.'

STABLE NOTES

PERSONAL DETAILS
17hh bay gelding, ⅞ Thoroughbred
Born 1985, by I'm a Star (TB) out of Omineen Model
Stable name 'Apple'

MAIN ACHIEVEMENTS
2nd Osberton 1991
2nd Punchestown 1993
4th Burghley 1994
1st Punchestown 1995
1st Scottish Open 1996
1st Burghley 1996
869 horse trials points
Short-listed for 1996 Olympics

CHARACTERISTICS
Like Policeman Plod at home; very steady and reliable out hacking; big-framed horse with a large head; very brave and strong, with a big heart

LIKES
Rolling; titbits; galloping and jumping – and laps of honour!

DISLIKES
Anyone touching his ears; his tummy being brushed, and his girth being done up; injections; any graze, however small, being treated – he snorts and quivers with fright!

I heard about Star Appeal from Bernice Alexander, from whose yard I had actually bought King William. She had promised to let me know if she came across any other good young horses – and true to her word, she rang me as soon as Star Appeal came her way. He had been bred in Ireland by a wonderful character called Michael McEvoy, a solid Irishman whose accent is so broad I can still barely understand him, and who hates writing so much that it has fallen on his daughter to maintain communication between us!

'I liked his attitude – he seemed to have a really fresh, jolly outlook and just seemed to love life.'

'As soon as I saw Apple I liked him – he was a lovely free-moving horse and looked extremely powerful. But he was already very big as a five-year-old, and I was a little worried as to how much bigger and heavier he might get. Nevertheless he had lovely limbs, good straight movement, and a careful, if not particularly stylish jump. Most of all I liked his attitude – he seemed to have a really fresh, jolly outlook and just seemed to love life. His jump felt fantastic when you rode him, although from the ground he didn't pick up his forelegs very well. However, my showjumper trainer at the time, Kenneth Clawson, felt that his jump was plenty good enough and so the Pinders kindly agreed to buy him for me.

'I did not push Apple's training in any way at all because he was such a big horse and the ground was hard that summer; we just took things quietly at home getting to know each other. The first event we went to was Llanfechain, and there I was amazed at the quality of his performance across country: he was so bold, yet very sensible and gave me a lovely smooth ride – it felt as if he had been doing it for years, although I knew he had not been across country at all. He was a true "natural".

'Dressage on the other hand was difficult for him, especially in trot as he found it hard to balance himself, although this gradually improved with quiet, steady schooling at home. I would use plenty of transitions to help push his hindquarters under him more; this in turn takes his weight off his forehand and makes it easier for him to balance and to carry himself. He qualified for the Novice Futurity Finals, a championship for five- and six-year-old horses that had been first or second in a novice horse trials that year. It was held at Tetbury over a demanding novice track, and Apple won it: this was most exciting as he was competing against six-year-olds with a great deal more experience than he had. He finished the season with about fifteen points, leaving me looking forward enthusiastically to the following year when, as a six-year-old, I felt we would really make progress.

'That second season he came out feeling very good indeed: he won a couple of novice events, and I felt he was quite ready to go up a step to intermediate – the jumping phases were obviously so easy for him it was just wonderful, although he continued to find the dressage difficult. At the end of that year he went to Osberton, his first three-day event and finished second there behind Conker. On the strength of these performances I felt confident to take him to Bramham the following spring. By this time his dressage was just starting to come together, and here he produced a good enough test at this level to put him in the top ten. But sadly he was denied the chance to prove himself across country, because a tiny cut on his fetlock became infected and his leg swelled rapidly so we were obliged to withdraw him. This was in 1992, and soon after that I went out to the Barcelona Olympics with William so there was little time to do much more with him that season.

'The plan for him in 1993, when he was eight, was to aim for the Punchestown three-day event; this is the same standard as Bramham but comes a little earlier in the spring. Everything went very well in his preparation, for his jumping was as good as ever, and his dressage was improving rapidly; as he matured and strengthened he was better able to handle himself and to maintain his balance in a test. He finished second at Punchestown with a performance that really caught the selectors' eye, and he was long listed, along with William, for the European Championships in Achselswang.

'I ran him at Montacute open intermediate as the first part of his build-up to the championships

Page 66: The Scottish Open Championships at Thirlestane saw Apple's first major success in his new noseband, which was part of a fantastic autumn run for Mary in 1996

– this was his first event since Punchestown. The ground was hard so I decided to take him quietly, and he felt super. But as I took off his overreach boots I noticed a spot of blood in the sole of his hoof; we scrubbed it clean but still couldn't see anything obviously wrong, so I assumed he head perhaps just trodden on a sharp stone. But the following day he was slightly unlevel, and he became increasingly lame over the next few days. The vet considered that something sharp had probably pierced the sole and come out again, and that as a result the foot had become infected, the abscess running along under the sole to cover quite a large area. He cut a hole in the sole to allow the pus to drain out, and we kept poulticing the foot to help draw out the infection.

'In spite of this treatment Apple did not get any better, and we were advised to take him to a specialist vet, Simon Grant, in Crewkerne; there, a dye was injected into the hole in the sole and the foot x-rayed, the purpose of this being that the dye would follow the path that the infection had taken, which could then be seen clearly on the x-ray. The dye seemed to branch out all over the place, although luckily the infection had not attacked the pedal bone. Unfortunately for Apple, however, the only way to let the bad matter out was to cut away a large piece of his frog, leaving him with a very painful wound; this then had a special shoe fitted over it with a plate that covered and protected the sensitive frog area. The plate screwed on and off, and we would remove it twice a day so that we could clean and dress the wound.

'...a week later, Apple suffered another but potentially much more damaging setback...'

'With time, Apple's foot recovered and we were able to resume his work again. He had obviously lost any chance of going to the European Championships, as had William who had blotted his copybook in the eyes of the selectors with another poor showjumping performance at Badminton earlier in the year. So I decided to take them both to Boekelo three-day event – but at the last minute this was cancelled because of torrential rain. So I had two fit horses all ready for a big party but nothing to go to; so we travelled to Bishop Burton College for the last advanced one-day event of the season, where Apple finished third. In a small way this helped to counter the disappointments of that season.

'By 1993 Apple's owners, the Pinders, had decided they wanted to sell Apple; they had become more involved in racing because this was their son's interest. I was loath to lose the ride on him – I had worked very hard on him and knew that his best was still to come, and although his career had been marred by injuries these were not his fault. After much discussion and negotiation, David and I bought him ourselves. And then just a week later, Apple suffered another, but potentially much more damaging setback to his eventing career: he was turned out as usual in the field with Conker when, in the course of some playful chasing around, Conker kicked out and caught him high up on his left forearm. It obviously just wasn't Apple's day, because the kick resulted in a star fracture of his leg.

'The only chance of successful treatment involved immobilising him for six weeks; this is very often done by putting the leg in plaster, although this in itself can cause problems because the leg can become badly rubbed and the muscle wastage is very great. My vet wanted to avoid these potential problems, so Apple was immobilised by two ropes attached one on each side of his headcollar and then tied to the ceiling; this meant he could move his quarters from side to side but could not lie down. The risk of him lying down was too great to take, because so much pressure is put on the front legs when a horse gets up, that the fractured bone might have shattered completely. During the first few days of his confinement he tried sitting down, then he tried kneeling down; but he soon realised it was impossible and settled down to be a very good patient. The hardest thing for him was that towards the end of the six weeks he obviously desperately wanted to roll even though there was no way that he could.

'He was x-rayed every fortnight throughout the six-week period, and luckily the fracture healed very satisfactorily. Initially the x-rays showed there was a little chip of bone floating around, but as the new bone grew it attached to that and was held safely where it could do no damage. During the last week I would go and sit with him every afternoon and count the days down with him, until on the very last night I could tell him that by the next day he would be free to move around again – and the following morning when I went to check him he had freed himself! His patience had finally given out and he had snapped the ropes and had rolled, and rolled, and rolled! He just looked so happy! But I don't like to think what might have been the outcome if he had managed to do this a few weeks earlier.

'His patience had finally given out and he had snapped the ropes and rolled, and rolled, and rolled!'

'Being virtually immobilised for six weeks had obviously left Apple very unfit. He had lost all his muscle tone, and when I led him out for his first short exercise in hand he was so excited that he hardly knew what to do with himself – he looked as if he had quite forgotten what he had to do with his legs in order to walk! His leg had been fractured in February, and after his initial six weeks' box-rest it took a further ten or twelve weeks to build up his fitness. He started by being led out for ten minutes twice a day, and this was gradually built up so that by the end of the first month he was being ridden out at walk for thirty to forty-five minutes a day. Then it was a case of building his fitness as you would for any horse, by making his rides longer, then including some trot, and finally an increasing amount of canter. Once he was strong enough to do some trotting, we also started to turn him out in the field again during the day so that he could exercise the leg himself as well. In spite of what could have been a fatal, if freak accident, I do still turn horses out together because the small amount of land I have doesn't really leave me any choice – and I still consider that it was incredibly bad luck that such an innocuous-looking incident led to such a bad injury.

'I entered him for the open intermediate at Lowesby that June and he felt every bit as good as before. His programme continued without a hitch until finally, after so many false starts, he got to Burghley where he would attempt a four-star competition for the first time. Although he felt slightly unsure of himself when he first encountered the really big fences, he soon settled into his stride and responded well to me. I didn't push him too fast, and he finished the event in fourth place, with Conker second. This was a most exciting moment, to feel confident that I now had two quality four-star horses to follow in William's footsteps.

'The following year, 1995, I was in the very happy position of having all three horses, William, Conker and Apple, qualified for Badminton. Each rider may only take two horses, and because my three all remained fit and well, I had to decide who to leave out; I definitely wanted to take William, so it was between Apple and Conker. Which horse I didn't take would go to Punchestown, and I knew that the event would suit Apple better than Conker. I felt totally confident that Apple would be capable of Badminton, but I wasn't quite so sure about Conker's bravery at the highest level; I was therefore keen to put that to the test, so I would at least know the calibre of horse we were dealing with from then on. So Apple went out to Punchestown, accompanied by David and a whole crowd of his friends who had decided to make the event his "stag weekend" as we were getting married the following

Above: Apple and Annie share a quiet moment at Punchestown in 1993

week! Apple gave us a brilliant early wedding present by winning the event, and it was especially gratifying that Michael McEvoy, his breeder, was there to see him win.

'Once again Apple had impressed the selectors and was long listed, together with William and Conker, for the 1995 Open European Championships that autumn. For once his preparation went very smoothly: he was second in the British Open Championship at Gatcombe, and was runner-up to William at the final trial in Scotland. But once again he was to be denied his moment of glory: during his cross-country round at the final trial I had felt him stumble slightly, and when we finished I found that he had over-reached quite badly and pulled off his shoe, leaving a nasty gash on his heel. But there was worse to come, because by the next day there was heat in his tendon and a scan showed that the suspensory ligament had taken a bit of a wrench. It was a very minor injury, but enough for him to miss the rest of the season. Poor Apple, it just seemed that every time he took a step forwards, something happened to knock him backwards again.

'The selectors had not lost interest, however, and over the winter months he joined the longlist for the 1996 Atlanta Olympics. At that time, if I had had to choose between Apple and William, I would have considered Apple to have been better suited to the conditions in Atlanta, so I was very excited about his prospects. He was now capable of a good dressage test, and his cross-country performances so far had matched William's, with the added bonus that he was an easier showjumper in the final phase.

'Apple gave us a brilliant wedding present by winning the event...'

'His warm-up for Badminton went very well, with good placings at his two advanced runs that spring, leaving me looking forwards to riding him more than ever there and having the chance, at long last, to show everyone what he was made of. Although his dressage was still probably his weakest phase, at Badminton he produced an admirable test to hold eighth place. He

Above: 'That feels *so* good...' Apple unwinds in typical fashion!

gave me a really good, smooth ride round the steeplechase phase and we set off on the cross-country with the highest of hopes. But again it was disaster: as we came to the first fence I realised we were going to meet it on a bad stride and I just froze a little; I didn't want to check him, as I had found from experience that if I could sit quietly and be very soft with my hands then he stays soft and settled,

but if I start defensively and take a hold of him to organise him in front of the fence then he just fights you the whole way. So I did not check him – but neither did I move him up to the fence to help him reach a better take-off point; I really thought that, being so bold and scopey, he would stand off and clear it easily. But he didn't – he chipped in a little stride which put him much too close to it, so then he did not get enough height to clear it. He hit it very hard with his front legs, and although he stayed on his feet, I was torpedoed into the ground and suffered a very heavy fall. I didn't feel fit enough to continue and so, unbelievably, our first Badminton ended at the first fence! I really thought the selectors would write him off after that, but obviously they felt that one mistake was forgivable; after all, it was the only *real* mistake he had ever made across country, and so he was given a second chance. I had to run him at Bramham three-day event a few weeks later if I still wanted him to be considered for an Olympic team place.

'We therefore entered him in the advanced class at Savernake Forest, the only run that he would have before Bramham. Unusually he became very strong, stronger than I had ever known him on a cross-country course – he seemed to be really wound up, probably as a result of the anti-climax of Badminton. In fact I felt we were lucky to survive without incident, and hoped that the run would have taken some of the edge off him. As a precaution I took him cross-country schooling to help me decide whether or not I needed to change his bit, but for this he behaved extremely well, and I felt confident that he was back to his smooth, controllable self.

'At Bramham he excelled in the dressage, but on speed and endurance day I found out too late that he was simply over the top as far as his fitness was concerned. He set off quietly enough but became increasingly strong, charging at the fences as soon as he sighted them. Any influence I might have had over him quickly vanished, and finally he was just running through the bridle and getting stronger and faster the further he went. Peter Scudamore, once champion National Hunt jockey, used to say: "If you're thinking about pulling up, then hurry up and pull up." And I wish I had taken that advice, because just as I was thinking that there was no way I would even want to be riding Apple in Atlanta if he was going to be so strong, he ran so fast and flat at the next fence, an upright gate, that he simply didn't get high enough to clear it. Once again he stayed on his feet but I was somersaulted through the air. I am convinced that Apple himself will never fall – he is so strong and powerful that while fences may come crashing down around him, he always seems to remain standing. But I also knew then that he was going to need some serious reschooling to get him back under control, so I took him home from Bramham and simply turned him out in the field – and it is an indication of just how fit and uptight he was that it wasn't until he had been out in the field for at least ten days that he even started to relax and let his muscles go.

'Apple was brought back into work while I was away at the Olympics, because I planned to take him to Burghley. Perhaps it was just as well that he

Above: Annie and Apple meet the fans at Badminton 1996

wasn't selected for the Olympic team: when I took William and Apple to Newmarket for them to be tested in the controlled environment trials being operated for the Olympic horses, William actually coped with the heat and humidity better than Apple. Apple sweated more copiously and his core temperature was higher than William's; so even if he had gone well at Bramham and been picked for Atlanta, he may well have ended up struggling in the conditions that will prevail there.'

An Autumn Challenge

'One of my first thoughts on returning from Atlanta was "Oh no, I've got to ride Apple again!" It wasn't really that bad, but after his disastrous cross-country performances at Badminton and Bramham I knew that I needed either to solve the problem of controlling him across country, or I would have to accept that he was too strong for me and sell him. Whilst in Atlanta I had discussed him with fellow riders Chris Hunnable and Ian Stark, both of whom had experience of very strong cross-country horses. Chris had suggested I try his "combination noseband", and Ian suggested a Dutch gag with a Waterford mouthpiece. The combination noseband lies slightly lower on the horse's nose than a normal cavesson, and has two metal half-moon pieces which sit in front of the bit and are held by straps which do up under the chin. The Waterford mouthpiece consists of several chunky links which wrap around the horse's mouth, and this is more comfortable for some horses than the nutcracker action of the normal snaffle mouthpiece.

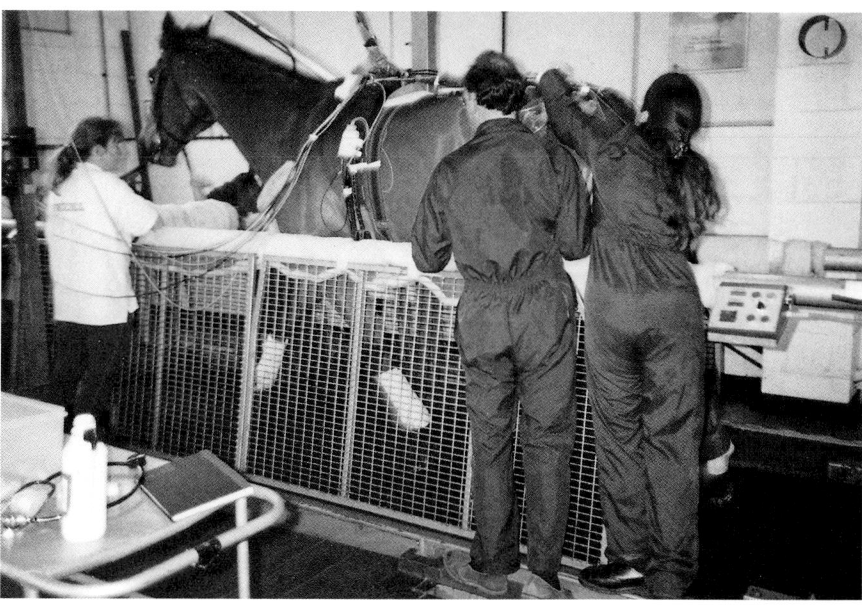

'I had entered Apple for the advanced class at Hartpury horse trials, held on the weekend after we returned from Atlanta, and made the positive decision that if I did not feel in control then I would pull him up and not continue. Prior to this, he had always been quite steady in his attitude on arrival at an event – but at Hartpury he was definitely very nervous and wound up, and this proved to me that he had been worried by his experiences in the spring. He did his dressage the day before, and for the rest of that day I spent quite a lot of time riding him round near the start of the cross-country course, until he relaxed and settled down. Then after his showjumping the following morning I took him straight back up to the cross-country start and worked him there again, before going to get ready for the cross-country. I knew that I would have to concentrate on being as light as possible with my hands so that he would not feel he was in any way restricted and then have an excuse to fight. I am sure a lot of his pulling in the past has been as a result of my trying to dominate him too much at the start of the course. As we proceeded round the Hartpury course he did start to get stronger; but on the whole he felt more controllable, and he showed more respect for the fences than he has done in the past. It was still far from perfect, but it was a big step in the right direction.

'Apple's next outing was the Scottish Open Championships at Thirlestane Castle. He produced a good dressage test to finish well up in his section,

Above left: Apple at Newmarket, undergoing the controlled environment trials for Olympic horses

and this was most encouraging – especially as we were up against many combinations which were also destined for Burghley. The cross-country is run before the showjumping in this championship, and so in the morning I gave Apple a good hack round and let him have a splash in the river which runs past the stables. However, when we went up to the cross-country start we found that there was a hold on the course, which led to a long wait; Apple started to get fairly uptight, and I knew that today would be a very good test of the new braking system. I had it in the back of my mind that I must leave him alone, and that I needed to look for *forward* strides to the fences, and *not* be tempted to keep trying to hook him back. He started very smoothly, and by the time he was thinking about getting strong we were amongst the more technical fences such as the coffin and the sunken road; thankfully he does respect this type of fence, and so he allowed me to set him up a little in front of them. He produced a fast clear across country, and then finished the competition with a good showjumping round to take the title.

'Gatcombe was the weekend before Burghley and I had only ever intended riding him across country there if things had gone wrong at Thirlestane. As it was, I was happy with the feel that he gave me in Scotland, and so we did only take part in the dressage and showjumping phases at Gatcombe.'

Burghley Horse Trials

'On the way up to Burghley we called in for a lesson with Ferdi Eilberg. Apple is not a natural dressage horse, finding it difficult to achieve the self-carriage that is needed to make him look impressive and elegant. On this occasion Ferdi actually rode him, and this was a great help; being that much stronger and more experienced than I, he was able to engage Apple's hindquarters far more than I can. This helped Apple to realise that he *can* carry himself, and that he doesn't need to be so reliant on the rider's hands for support.

'Our dressage was on the first afternoon of Burghley, and Apple really did try very hard. His test was good enough to take the lead, and he was only equalled on the second day by Bruce Davidson. Although there was still a long way to go, for me this was the most rewarding part of the whole event. As I have said, Apple has always found this phase the most difficult, and he had shown a real improvement.

'Having had such a good ride at Thirlestane, I was looking forward to the challenge of Saturday's cross-country. I was quite decided to pull up if I found him getting too strong, but felt that if we survived the steeplechase then we would cope with the rest. Sure enough, he did get very strong on the steeplechase – he has a massive, ground-covering stride and was loving every minute of it – but although I *knew* he was going faster than we needed, he was jumping sensibly. We finished well inside the time, and although this, as a rule, is nothing to be proud of, with him I knew it was safer *not* to restrict him in any way. When we arrived at the ten-minute halt box again there was a hold on the course, and we had to wait for forty-five minutes. This time, however, it probably worked in our favour, because I am sure Apple thought he had finished for the day. As it got close to re-starting, the other riders were busy trying to wake their horses up again to get them switched back on to the job in hand. But I only did enough with Apple to be sure his muscles were warmed up since I wanted to keep him as calm as possible.

'He set off well, and settled quickly into a good, strong galloping stride, yet I had enough control to ride the turns accurately and smoothly, which always helps you to achieve a good time across country. We had only one anxious moment: I knew the sunken road would be a difficult fence for Apple, as it was a tight one stride in the bottom and then only three strides to a big corner once you had jumped up out of the road. I had decided that if anything felt wrong as we went through the sunken road, then I would have to act quickly to pull out to the side to take the alternative route rather than the corner. Apple did trip slightly coming up out of the road, but I was delighted to find how easily he let me turn him away from the corner and round the alternative route. Again, he did just start to get strong towards the end of the course, but it was still well within acceptable limits.

'Apple kept his lead after the cross-country – our joint leader after the dressage, Bruce Davidson, had had a fall on the cross-country course – and our nearest rival now was Andrew Nicholson; we had just one showjumping fence in hand over him. Andrew produced a masterful round out of his horse which seemed determined to make the minimal effort over each fence, but they had the very last one down which gave us a little more breathing space. Apple used up one of the fences we had in hand, but he did enough to claim victory.

'I was so thrilled for him; he has had so many false starts in his career, but this time it all came together. I had been second at Burghley twice before, so the ultimate prize this time was very sweet. Apple finished the event feeling very fit and sound, and I felt far more confident about his future.'

Annie on Star Appeal

'When Apple arrived in the yard he was no more than a big, floppy baby – he hardly seemed in control of his long legs – generally gentle, but occasionally boisterous. One of my first abiding memories of him was when we decided to take him to Bramham with us. William was competing there, and because Mary hadn't had Apple very long and wanted to spend some time getting to know him, we were given permission to stable him at the event so that she could ride him each day. And far from being overawed or getting silly and excited, he spent most of the time asleep! He would lie flat out on one side, then stand up and have a good shake before lying flat out on the other side. Whenever Mary sent me to get him ready for her to ride he was sleeping!

'Now that he is older he is far from floppy, and in fact is very strong and solid; we always say he should have been a police horse because he just keeps marching on through whatever might be in the way. It's a case of "Come on Mum, let's go

Right: Triumph at Burghley: the showjumping round was followed by Mary's usual celebratory lap of honour and later, a smiling Mary shows off her trophy

straight through that crowd" or..."straight over that car". I love him dearly because he is such a character in that respect. He is a super horse to look after, but has been unlucky in that various injuries have held him back throughout his career – although he has always been a very good patient. He lives in the biggest stable in the yard and makes sure he uses every inch of it, so the only drawback to "doing" him is that his bed takes a lot of work to keep it tidy. But in every other respect – to hack and to lead out, to groom and generally tidy up – he is brilliant: that is, apart from his ears. He just won't let me near them, and his adamant refusal is one of the few behaviour traits I have not been able to conquer during my grooming career – and I am not sure that I ever will. Even so, he is a most attractive sort of horse to have in the yard; it's rather like having another Boris.

'He was so laid back...when I went to get him ready for the trot-up he was sound asleep!'

'I remember travelling out with him to the Punchestown three-day event, where everyone else in the stabling area nicknamed him PC Plod because he was so laid back, just as at Bramham; when I went to get him ready for the trot-up he was sound asleep! But he had his revenge when he won it! My favourite event with him was Burghley in 1994. That year we hadn't had a particularly good season at all, and although we knew that both Conker and Apple were future super stars, we weren't really sure how they would cope with an event of this calibre. But both horses gave 100 per cent: Apple is not as capable physically as Conker, and so he always has to try that bit harder to succeed; so he really deserved his fourth place. And at the start of 1996 he once again found himself somewhat in William's shadow, particularly as things went very wrong for him early in the season: he hit the first fence at Badminton so hard that Mary was thrown off, and then he ran away with her at Bramham, walloped another fence and sent her cartwheeling again. But the fact that his middle name is "Try" was certainly proved at Thirlestane and Burghley, when all our dreams for him came true at last!

'Although Burghley is a very exciting event to be at, it was far more relaxing for me being in charge of Star Appeal than ever it is trying to look after William at a three-day event. William is very much a 'home boy' and becomes unsettled in new surroundings; also, he usually immediately falls madly in love with whoever happens to be stabled next to him, and becomes ever more anxious each time that particular horse leaves its stable. Apple, on the other hand, is a far more laid-back character, who quickly settles into a new home and is so full of confidence that he soon forgets his manners. Thus William may be a worrier, but he is always a gentleman, whereas Apple can be a bit of a thug, especially if you have to lead him out. He seems to forget completely that I happen to be on the other end of the leadrope, and just thinks "Let's go and eat that bit of grass over there"; or, "Let's go and say hello to so-and-so in the next field" and just tows me along ignominiously.

'He has always been very much in William's shadow, and so when he went into the dressage arena at Burghley and produced such a good test I was really pleased for him. He is not extravagant – he just went in there and got on with it. All his work looked crisp and neat, and for a horse that genuinely finds this phase difficult, it was very rewarding.

'I have to admit that I was really nervous about what might happen on cross-country day. He and Mary had both been lucky not to have been badly hurt by the mistakes he made in the spring and part of me hoped she would come into the ten-minute box and withdraw him. But once I saw him behaving well on the steeplechase I started to relax. He was fast, but only because that happened to be his comfortable cruising speed. He jumped sensibly, and wasn't fighting for his head, and once he was over the first few fences I started to really enjoy watching him. He was in a good strong rhythm, but he was still listening to Mary, and finished looking really well with no signs of feeling in the least jarred up.

'He trotted up very well the next day, and then we just had to wait for the showjumping. Since having worked with William I am *always* nervous about the showjumping now. But I could see Apple was really trying, and when he won it was just so good that *at last* he was a real champion in his own right.'

The RISING STARS

Solly happy and confident at Portman early in the 1996 season, a quiet preparatory run before tackling the advanced class at Belton

92

‘I bought Solomon from a lady called Mary-Rose Weston, who lived near Cirencester. A friend of mine, Lisa Rowlands, was working in her yard and told me they had a very nice young horse there which might be coming up for sale.

SOLOMON III

I knew he would be competing at Gatcombe in the Burghley Young Event Horse class, so I made a point of watching him – and although he was quite naughty I did like the look of him; I therefore arranged to go and see him the following day. He looked much more a true Thoroughbred than any of my other horses, but that was the type I had started to look for: in recent years the lighter, more agile sort has shown they cope far better with the hard ground and hot, humid conditions so often associated with major championships these days.’

STABLE NOTES

PERSONAL DETAILS

16.1½hh bay gelding

Born 1988, by HIS stallion Old Lucky out of a near-TB mare – his great-grand-dam was a spotted cob!

Stable name ‘Solly’

MAIN ACHIEVEMENTS

2nd Le Lion d'Angers 1994

1st Frizzell British Novice 1994

1st Compiègne 1995

1st Ladies Open Advanced Thirlestane 1996

2nd British Open Gatcombe 1996

1st Blenheim 1996

353 horse trials points

CHARACTERISTICS

Very happy sort of character; extremely intelligent, and very talented; finds everything easy

LIKES

Jumping; competing; being turned out; loves rolling; sticking his tongue out and flapping it around at feed time; chewing his haynet when empty

DISLIKES

Pretends he sees things in the hedge and gallops off in the opposite direction; being caught if he hasn't had long enough in the field

He moved well and had a careful, if "green" jump. It was obvious that he was quite a naughty character, but I was fairly confident that, as he was only five, I could turn him around without too much trouble and channel his exuberance into his work rather than into misbehaving. Once he was in our yard his favourite trick, especially if the girls were riding him, was to whip round and then buck and buck until they fell off. Although he never managed to unseat *me,* it wasn't safe to let him continue doing this, as the girls often have to ride him out. So once he had had a week or two to settle in, I determined to sort it out and took him on exercise myself: as expected, he whipped round and started bucking – except that this time he was punished with the whip and given a good scolding, a procedure which thoroughly shocked him, I think. Throughout his education up to that point allowances had been made for the fact that he was only young – but he had started to take advantage of that, and it was time he was told where he had to draw the line. He only bucked once after that, and although he is still prone to whipping round, he does it less often.

'As it was quite late in the season when I bought him, there was only time to take him to a couple of events as a five-year-old: he did the pre-novice at Upton House, and then a novice class at Lulworth where he was fifth, and so finished his first short season with two points. Although I had had him only a short time, it was very obvious that he was a far more careful horse than any of my others. Although he enjoyed the cross-country he was very deliberate about what he did, and was especially wary of ditches and water. So I knew he was not a horse to rush – he would need time to learn his job well and to trust me.

'...his favourite trick...was to whip round and then buck and buck until they fell off.'

'During his preparation for his next season I spent a lot of time letting him "play" over ditches and in water. He had really matured over the winter and as a six-year-old looked far more "up together". When I bought him he had a really big, high bottom, and when he jumped he would throw his back end right out behind him which then pitched him very much on his forehand; but through the winter his front end had come up to match his hindquarters, and he was looking really good. That spring he won four novice events in a row. He was performing lovely dressage tests and was feeling extremely confident across country. He tackled his first intermediate at Lowesby which he did easily and smoothly. After a short holiday, our intention was to run him in a number of intermediates to qualify him for his first three-day event: Le Lion d'Angers. Everything went smoothly: his dressage was steadily improving, he was a naturally careful jumper and seemed genuinely to enjoy the cross-country. I did find he was starting to get quite strong and so tried him in a pelham bit; this helped me to control him on the cross-country and also kept him lighter on his forehand in the showjumping.

'At Le Lion d'Angers he performed really well, keeping up with the older horses that were com-

Page 106: Mary and Solly on their way to Mary's fourth major win in a row at Blenheim 1996

peting against him. He was second after the dressage, and in spite of the pouring rain on cross-country day, tackled the course comfortably. A super clear round in the showjumping held second place for him – he was beaten by an older, more experienced horse, Darien Powers, ridden by Andrew Hoy and later to be part of the Australian gold medal-winning team at the Atlanta Olympics. At Le Lion d'Angers there is a prize for the highest-placed six-year-old horse, and this went to Solomon. As a seven-year-old I planned to take him to Compiègne, which was the same standard as at Le Lion d'Angers. Although William had gone straight to Bramham as a seven-year-old, I did not think that Solomon was quite ready for that challenge, and my doubts seemed to be justified because before going to Compiègne I entered him for his first advanced where he gave me a real shock by stopping at the coffin! He did jump it at the second attempt, and seemed very happy tackling the rest of the course; but I felt glad I was not taking him staight to Bramham. At Compiègne he led from the start: he was clear and inside the time across country, and showjumped clear to retain his lead and win overall. His future was starting to look very exciting.

'At Le Lion d'Angers Solomon took the prize for the highest-placed six-year-old.'

'The plan was to compete him at Blenheim that autumn; this would be a step up from the previous three-day events he had tackled. However, the ground had become extremely hard, besides which I was determined to take him very carefully during his preparation. He had upgraded to advanced by now, and so competed in one open intermediate class before going to Gatcombe and Thirlestane to do the advanced. At both these events he felt really happy and confident across country: at Gatcombe I took him quietly, but at Thirlestane we pressed on a little bit faster to finish in the top ten. Unfortunately our plans were thwarted because just before leaving for Blenheim I felt a suspicion of heat in his front leg and he was just slightly unlevel. Up to this point he had proved to be a very tough and

sound horse, so I did not feel it was worth the risk of rushing to get him better. We called it a day and turned him out for his holiday.

'In 1996 the aim was to take him to Bramham. He therefore had two open intermediate runs and then went to the advanced at Belton, where the showjumping track was huge; however, he coped well and was clear. At Bicton advanced we decided to be a bit more competitive and pressed on across country to finish in second place. He then won the OI at Lanhydrock and so our preparation so far was going well. But during his last gallop before leaving for Bramham he started to cough. We took his temperature three times a day over the next few days and it didn't alter, although he continued to cough. The day we were due to leave for the event he also had a runny, mucky nose. My vet was happy for us to take him up there, but advised us to tell the vets on arrival and ask to be put in an isolation box – the feeling was that as his temperature hadn't altered, he was probably having an

Left and above: Mary celebrates her Gatcombe triumph: first place with William and second with Solly

allergic reaction to something. Once at Bramham his temperature still didn't alter so we were allowed to go ahead. He performed a good dressage test but it did lack sparkle, and when we took his temperature afterwards it had gone up; moreover he then began to cough even more, and both his eyes and nose were runny. It was obvious now that he did have some sort of flu virus and so we took him straight home; and to avoid the risk of any contact with the other horses, we didn't even take him into our yard but turned him straight into a field. He needed a few weeks' holiday, but then came back into work and seemed fully recovered.'

Autumn Campaign

'My intention all season with Solomon was to enter him for the Blenheim three-day event in the autumn, so while I was away in Atlanta, Becky was at home getting him fit ready for the autumn. He was entered for the advanced intermediate class at Hartpury, where he proved to be a joy to ride, producing a lovely dressage test and showjumping clear, and then he felt really good across country. The going had become quite deep in the wooded areas so I took him round steadily and he finished in sixth place.

'His next outing was in one of the advanced sections at Thirlestane Castle. Again he produced a truly lovely dressage test which I was really pleased with, but when I looked at the scoreboard he had been given a mark of only 38! I couldn't believe it – more and more marks went up that were better than his, and I didn't know what to think. Had I been there on my own I would probably have left it at that, and assumed that although the test felt good, the judge obviously hadn't liked it; but Gill Robinson was with me, and she was determined that our score should be checked. And how lucky that she insisted, because when his dressage sheet *was* rechecked, it was discovered that they *had* in fact made a mistake: Solly had scored 28, and this immediately took the lead.

'Having regained some advantage I was determined to make the most of it on the cross-country. I had always thought of Solly as the baby, but I knew it was time to ask a bit more of him. He responded brilliantly, and felt really grown up and confident. He won the section by a good margin, giving me a great start to a great day, because I won the championship class in the afternoon with Apple.

'We went to Gatcombe feeling very confident. I knew I would need a good score in the dressage, and although Solly usually scores well, he still works rather longer and lower than he ought to at this level; he is quite lazy at heart, and is happy to let his rider do all the work while he does as little as he can get away with. So I was very conscious of making sure he really *was* awake, and sharp off my leg. He did produce a good test which held third place behind William, and then showjumped clear and moved up to second place, overtaking Willie, who had had a fence down. By the time I rode Solly across country, I had already recorded a fast clear with William. I did not want to rush Solomon as he still had Blenheim to come, so I settled for a comfortable round. As it turned out, he was only five time faults slower than William, so I knew I had a potentially fast horse on my hands; and whilst William took first place, Solly was quite happy to settle for the runner-up spot!

'...when his dressage sheet *was* rechecked, it was discovered that they *had* made a mistake.'

'So his preparation for Blenheim, which was to be his first three-star event, couldn't have gone better.

'As a final preparation we stopped off for a lesson with Ferdi Eilberg on the way to Blenheim – and Ferdi really inspired me to insist that Solly put *more* into his work, encouraging me to ride him much more strongly so that he performed the movements with more expression and flair.

'I put all this into practice at Blenheim, insisting that Solly respond quickly and sharply to my leg aids, and making sure that he did not lean on my hand as a way of rebalancing himself. When he entered the arena he felt lighter in my hand than he had done previously, and he was beginning to adopt the more advanced outline which is needed at this level. It all comes down to him being prepared to work a bit harder so that he lowers his hindquarters and steps underneath himself further with his hindlegs, which in turn

Above: Solly maintaining good relations with his owner

raises and lightens his forehand, producing a higher, more compact outline. He took the lead in this phase, but what was more exciting was that now I knew there was even better work to come from him, and that next season he would be an even more impressive horse.

'I had a busy few days at Blenheim because I had to act as my own groom, Annie having had to stay at home until Friday night to look after the other horses as we were short-staffed. It was a very long time since I had had to do my own plaiting, and I was so relieved when they all stayed in place throughout the vet's inspection and the dressage! Annie would never have forgiven me otherwise. However, I nearly did completely disgrace myself when, still in sole charge of Solomon one afternoon, I decided to lead him out to graze. After a while I fancied a cup of coffee, to I tied him up to the side of the lorry on a long length of leadrope so that he could continue to graze. I kept spying on him through the lorry window and he seemed perfectly happy. But all at once there was a tremendous commotion, and I dashed out to see that he had put his leg over the rope and then thrown his head up, so that the rope was now pulled tight and his leg was hooked over it. Just as I got to him the string snapped and he broke free, but the rope had burned the skin on the inside of his knee. I couldn't believe I could have been so stupid as to have left him unattended like that, and could just imagine what *I* would have said to Annie if *she* had ever done such a thing! I hosed the leg and kept icepacks on it to keep any swelling to a minimum, and luckily for me it did not affect him at all. Needless to say, I was *very* glad indeed to see Annie when she arrived on Friday!

'...I could just imagine what *I* would have said to Annie is *she* had ever done such a thing!'

'For the first time the cross-country was run in reverse order of dressage scores – so we were the last to go, which made it very nerve-racking but far more exciting. It was a very stiff three-star course, and it was certainly going to be a big step up for Solomon. Having seen the course ride throughout the day, I knew I could only afford to take one or two long routes if I wanted to get a good enough time to keep my lead. There were several places where I would have liked the luxury of going the long way, but I knew that to win I couldn't afford to play safe.

'The going on the steeplechase was very hard and stony, and although Solly went round inside the time I could feel that it had jarred him up slightly. I was glad when he seemed to settle down and free up a bit on Phase C. He was very calm and collected in the ten-minute box, so when it was our turn to go we were both composed for the task ahead – or so I thought. In fact as we galloped to the first fence I could feel Solomon backing right down – his eyes were on stalks, and for whatever reason, he was extremely wary of what was really a very straightforward fence. I kept driving him forwards, but he was so suspicious of it that he jumped up onto the flowerbed apron, and then had to catjump over the rail that was suspended above it, instead of jumping the whole thing in one. Solly is a very careful horse and this really shook us both up, and as a result he took a while to settle into his stride, which was unfortunate because at this level the questions come up thick and fast. He was still 'looky' when we came to the first water, and wasn't as fluent as I would have liked; so at the next fence, a narrow S fence in the arena, I took the long route. I knew this would restrict my options later on, but he did not feel settled enough to tackle it.

'As we went on his confidence began to flow back, but I still found I was having to give him a smack with the stick in between fences just to keep him up in front of my leg. I didn't like doing this, especially as I could hear the crowd of spectators running from fence to fence behind us, but I knew I needed to keep him jumping forwards into my hand, not falling back and worrying about what was to come. He jumped very big over the double of logs into the first lake crossing, and jumped well over the fence actually in the water, but as we came to the step out, which was followed by a curved brush fence, I could feel that he was really being quite spooky again, so as we came up the step I pulled him out to the side and took the alternative. Now I knew I would have to press on and make up some of the time we had lost, and all the time we were getting closer and closer to the last serious question on the course, a big double of corners. By the time we were approaching it I knew that if I played safe and went the long way then we would be too slow to retain our lead – so we went for it, and he jumped beautifully through the combination. We finished with just over four points in hand, so it was very tight – and it also meant we did not have the luxury of a showjump in hand.

'Solly trotted up sound and well the next day, as did all our nearest rivals, so now it was down to what happened in the showjumping. Andrew Nicholson jumped a clear round so I knew I couldn't afford even one fence down. Solly jumped well, but he did just roll a pole in one of the combinations and so I assumed we had lost our lead – but then I suddenly realised from all the cheers that for some reason we hadn't. What had in fact happened was that although Andrew had jumped clear, he had incurred a time penalty and so we had won by a margin of 0.15 penalties!

'After the most bitter of disappointments in Atlanta it was hard to believe that only a few weeks later we could be enjoying such a wonderful run of success. But that's what the sport is all about: in Atlanta it was someone else's turn, now it was mine!

'I rate Solly very highly, and believe he is one of the best horses I have ever had – but I do know that he still needs to be tested over some of the really big tracks. As I have said, he is a very careful jumper, and this makes him rather more spooky across country than my previous horses, so I can't afford to rush him. But in the long term I think he will be spot-on to ride at the Sydney Olympics in the year 2000! '

Gill on Solly

'When I first saw King Solomon even I thought "Wow, we have a touch of class here!". He wasn't Mary's usual type of horse, being smaller and finer, but he has such a beautiful head. At home in the yard he is very amenable to deal with, but at events he becomes quite aloof – if you talk to him he tends to stare into space. Even so, just occasionally a certain amount of insecurity shows through, and then he obviously wants you to stay with him. I am sure he has a great future ahead of him.'

Annie on Solly

'When Solly came into the yard my first thought was "What a gorgeous young horse!" – and as a bonus, he was just my size! He was very well mannered in the yard, and apart from having a huge buck – which Mary had to teach him not to do before we could ride him – he was lovely in all respects. Right from day one there was just something about him which convinced you he was going to be an extremely good horse. He has matured considerably this year [1996], and was definitely much sharper when he came back into work in January: on the second day I rode him he saw something in the hedge and spun round, leaving me flat on my backside in the middle of the lane. I have decided that I really must be getting older and more sensible because I now prefer to have someone else with me when I ride him. So far in his career his biggest events have been Le Lion D'Angers, Compiègne and Blenheim, and he came second at Le Lion, which was immensely exciting as he was then still only six years old. We had already had a good result at Burghley with Conker and Apple, and there we were discovering that we had yet another top-class prospect for the future.

'When I first saw Solomon even I thought "Wow, we have a touch of class here!"'

'Solomon is a very placid workmanlike character; he prefers to know what is expected of him, and then to be allowed to settle down and concentrate on the work required. Obviously this attitude makes him thoroughly reliable and easy to ride in his competitions. He won at Compiègne as a seven-year-old and was all set for an exciting debut at Bramham in 1996 – but luck was not with us, unfortunately, because he developed a respiratory allergy after the first phase and could not continue; and to add to our disappointment Apple failed to impress the selectors – or any of us – when he galloped off with Mary on the cross-country and hit a fence so hard that she was thrown off. But Solomon is still very young, and his win at Blenheim makes him an exciting prospect for the future.'

'Lillie has filled a greatly honoured space in my eventing string: she is the first mare that I have ever bought. I was looking for another young horse and had rung round a few of my "faithful" contacts who know the sort of thing I like.

KING'S MISTRESS

Lillie was actually bred and owned by some friends of mine, John and Jane Poole, from whom I had bought a horse a few years before. They said they had one that they were sure I would like; I was looking for a 16.1hh gelding – they offered a 16.3hh mare! But they persuaded me to come and see her if I had time, and soon after, a trip to Stoneleigh provided the opportunity to call in at their Worcestershire stud.'

STABLE NOTES

PERSONAL DETAILS
16.3hh grey mare
Born 1991, by Louella Inschallah II out of Solo Love (TB)
Stable name 'Lillie'

MAIN ACHIEVEMENTS
1st Killerton Novice 1996
12 horse trials points

CHARACTERISTICS
Typical lady: loves being fussed over and pampered; very gentle to handle, but onward bound to ride; very beautiful and elegant

LIKES
Likes to let you know when she has had enough of being in the field – she comes to the gate and starts trying to open it when she is ready to come in!; being groomed and fussed around

DISLIKES
Being on her own (no-one to gossip with!); donkeys (but getting used to them)

I WAS SIX MONTHS PREGNANT with Emily and not really in a fit state to do too much, but I was very impressed with what I saw. For some reason I just hadn't expected her to be as attractive as she was, and when I actually saw her, I thought she was beautiful. She had superb natural paces and a lovely loose action, and when John popped her over some fences for me she proved to have a huge jump. I went back a few days later and rode her myself; I really liked the feel she gave me, so took the plunge and for the first time ever, bought a mare.

'I had already bought a young Irish horse, King Harry, so I worked them for a good month while the "big boys" were having their end-of-season rest. Neither had done much in the way of hacking out, so in those few weeks they were ridden out, taken over a few tiny logs and ditches, walked down into the local stream to introduce them to water and popped over some little jumps in the school. I also taught them to lunge correctly and obediently so that Annie could carry on with this sort of work once I was unable to ride. I was then whisked off on holiday by David – this was the only way he could make me stop riding as Emily's expected birth date crept ever closer! The two youngsters were turned out for a month before being brought back into work with the other horses in the New Year; they joined in the roadwork with the older horses and were lunged in between. Emily was born at the end of January and I was back riding very soon after that.

'Emily was born at the end of January and I was back riding very soon after that.'

'Lillie was aimed at the Portman pre-novice event; it was about a third of the way through the spring season, and a cross-country course which I know is not too demanding as an introductory event. I continued with her preparation, aiming to establish the basics in her flatwork and jumping. She is very forward thinking, and needed to understand that she must wait for her rider to ask her to do things, and not just go forging ahead under her own steam. She has a really big stride, and storms forwards with her head held high and her huge ears pricked – you feel a bit like a water skier being towed along behind! In this respect she is very like King William who always needed reminding to wait for me. So her work involved encouraging her to settle in a slow but consistent rhythm and in a long, low outline.

'In her jumping she also needed to slow down and take things calmly – whenever she saw a fence she tended to swing her head from side to side in order to free herself of the rein contact, and then just launched herself at it. However, as this was done as a result of enthusiasm rather than nerves, I wasn't worried about it at all. By the end of February she was ready to go indoor showjump-

ing, where she tackled a small novice track; she was quite spooky and had a couple of stops, but only through greenness. I took her jumping quite regularly after that and she soon settled down, and the more she did, the more she showed me that she had a lovely attitude and a very big jump.

'By the time the Portman came round she was really only just ready for it. However, in spite of her enthusiasm we managed to stay in the dressage arena throughout the test and earned a score of 27. She then wobbled her way round the showjumping, the phase where her greenness is the most evident; though as she progressed round the course she became straighter and steadier in her rhythm, and despite her inexperience, jumped clear, as she gives all her fences tremendous height.

'Across country she showed a really positive attitude and her only mistake was really my fault. I left it a bit late to get her on a line to a step coming up out of a field – a green horse takes more time to turn than an experienced one – and she stopped, but I didn't blame her for that. Other than that, she jumped clear.

'At Stockland Lovell pre-novice she led the dressage, showjumped clear and again gave me great confidence in her cross-country. She did stop at the rails in front of the sunken road, but this was entirely due to inexperience. I had brought her back to trot so that she could see what was coming after the rail – but having stopped, it seemed she couldn't take her eyes off the sunken road: she just kept staring at it and swished her tail a bit; but after a tap with the stick she went forwards again and jumped it well.

'Her next outing was Llanhydrock pre-novice, and here all the training came together with a good dressage and a double clear.

'Savernake Forest was her first novice outing. Although this is quite a big, testing track it is beautifully and fairly built. I could feel a real improvement in her dressage: she was working through from behind with much better engagement and was more balanced, and as a result was more ridable in the confines of the arena. Her showjumping was also more fluent, and she went beautifully across country to finish twelfth.

'...she is definitely different to the "boys", and can be quite a little tart in the yard!'

'I do stop running the younger horses once the ground gets too hard in the summer; they have a holiday and come back ready to tackle some of the autumn events. Lulworth horse trials were remarkably successful for Lillie: she managed to record an amazing dressage score of only 10, and then jumped a double clear to win her section. Her test felt really superb, and she is still only a novice! So her future looks very exciting. In her six-year-old season she will be properly competitive at this level, and as soon as she is making it all feel easy she will be upgraded to intermediate.

'Lillie has fitted into the yard really well. She is the first four-year-old I have bought, the first mare I have bought, and on top of that, she is grey which horrified Annie more than anything else. But as she loves being groomed and fussed around, that hasn't been a problem. Although she is not as temperamental as I had feared she might be, she is definitely different to "the boys", and can be quite a little tart in the yard! However, by the end of her next season we should have a better idea of what she is made of – and by the feel of things so far she is probably going to be a tiger across country!'

Above: Lillie on the pre-novice at her first event, at Portman. Her inexperience is shown by the fact that her front legs are not neatly tucked up together

Annie on Lillie

'We had never had a mare in the yard before Lillie; you do hear stories about mares being difficult to deal with when they are in season, and having a less even temperament than geldings, but Lillie is such a super-looking horse that I think Mary decided to ignore all her previous concerns and give her the benefit of the doubt. And there are far more mares competing anyway, these days, which gives people more confidence about trying a mare for themselves.

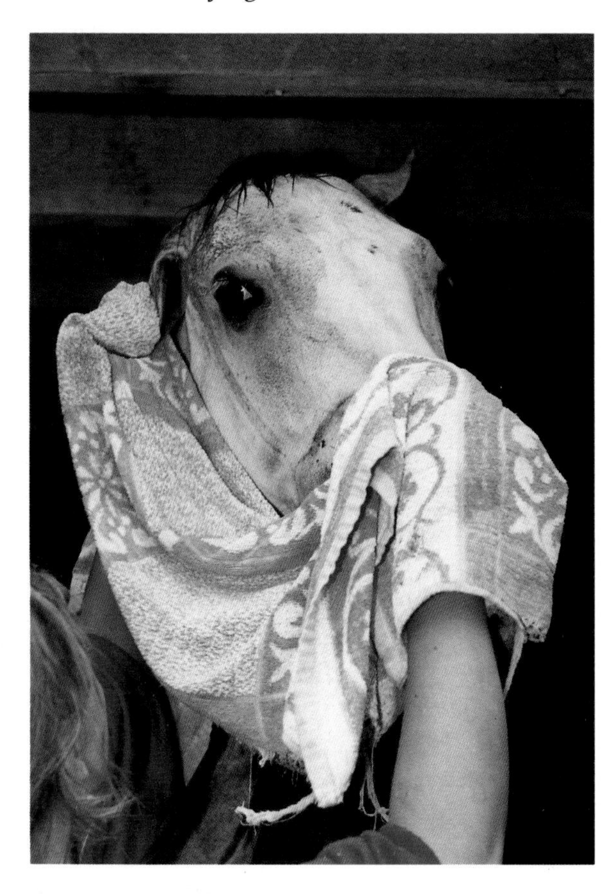

'Whilst the geldings all have varying characters, Lillie is different in another way – she is extremely sweet and gentle, but I know Mary has found that certainly as regards schooling, she is much happier if you *ask*, rather than tell her to do things. In the yard I suppose she does cause more of a commotion amongst the other horses than any of the geldings would on their own. She wants to flirt with everybody, which all the boys enjoy, but then they end up arguing with each other, and become really quite possessive about her! Henry is feeling like top dog at the moment as he is turned out at night with her!

'She is quite demanding in funny little ways – for example, when she has had a drink of water from her bucket and it is nearly empty she will tip what is left out as if to say, 'Hurry up girl, bring me more to drink!'. And she expects the boys to return her affections: she was obviously chasing after poor old Cuthbert in the field the other day, and being such a gentleman he was ignoring her advances – so she chased him right through the fence, which gave him a bit of a shock! As they say, there is nothing quite like a woman scorned!

'It does take more work to keep her clean, simply because she is grey. Any marks show up far more obviously, and whereas you can wash and shampoo the others the night before an event, you know that you will have to give Lillie another shampoo in the morning, to remove any stable stains; but she does look stunning when you finish!'

Gill on Lillie

'Lillie would be a really classy broad, perhaps an Elle MacPherson. She is quite a little madam, and I can just see her stamping her feet and saying "I want..." At the same time she is so elegant, and I can't wait to see her at advanced level with Mary in top hat and tails. In my opinion she is very brave, although Mary has conceded that you do have to ask her to do things, it's no good telling her. But then again, what female does like being told what to do? Even my husband Geoff was lost for words when he saw her; she really is very beautiful and Geoff isn't usually at all sentimental about horses. When I used to tell him how handsome William was, he would laugh and say, "How can a horse be handsome, for goodness sake?" But he does think Lillie is lovely! I am sure she will be with Mary for a very long time competing, but even so, I am already looking forward to breeding from her in the future.'

Sadly, just as Lillie was being brought back into work during the winter of 1996, she severed a front tendon – a self-inflicted wound – and so her competitive career was, tragically, finished.

A day in the life of
THE EVENT GROOM

William obviously finds Annie to be a very good rubbing post!

The team go to Hartpury 1996

1

2

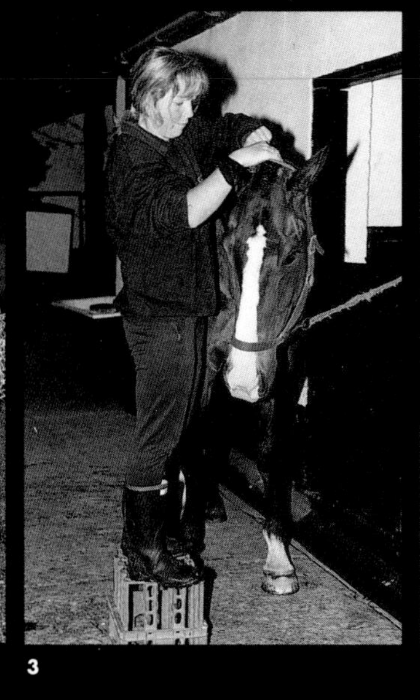

3

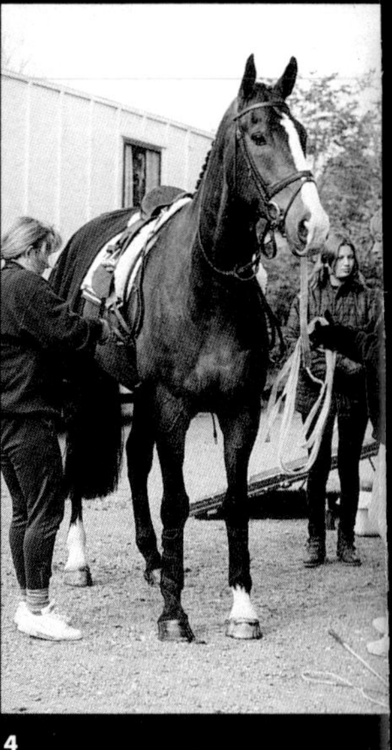

4

1 It's 4am and Annie is bringing William in from the field
2 Loading the haynets into the lorry
3 It's just starting to get light, and Annie is tidying William before the team set off. Note the famous milk crate – essential for that extra height!
4 8.30 and the team arrive at Hartpury. Mary attaches side reins so that William can be lunged in preparation for the dressage
5 After a satisfactory dressage test Gill gives William an affectionate nuzzle, while Annie untacks him
6 Annie cleaned the dressage saddle and put it away straight after the test to save having to do it in the lorry on the way home
7 Mary and Emily perform an outstanding extended trot during the course walk...
8 ...while Annie tackles one of the more difficult obstacles with Gill bringing up the rear!

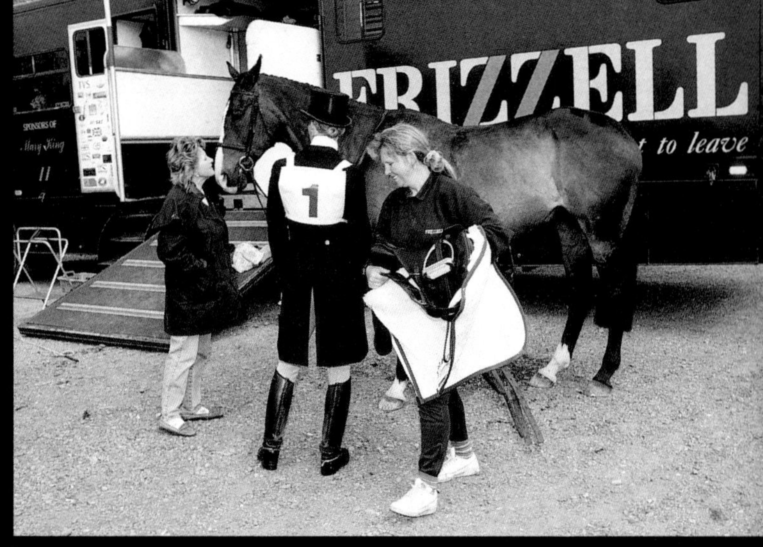

5

6

7

8

9

10

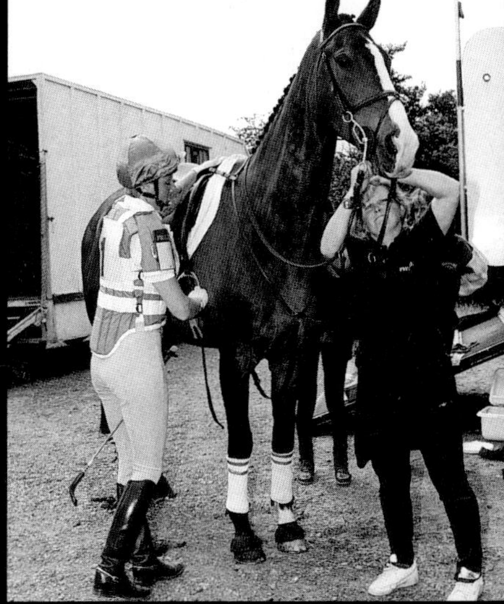

11

9 Lunch break and time to catch up on what's happening at home
10 Annie always leaves the front bandages for Mary to put on
11 Mary and Annie make the vital last checks before the cross-country
12 Annie always makes a point of being there to see that Mary gets off to a good start
13 Mary weighs in after the cross-country
14 William is no stranger to performing for the cameras, as he shows here!
15 The nail-biting showjumping phase

12

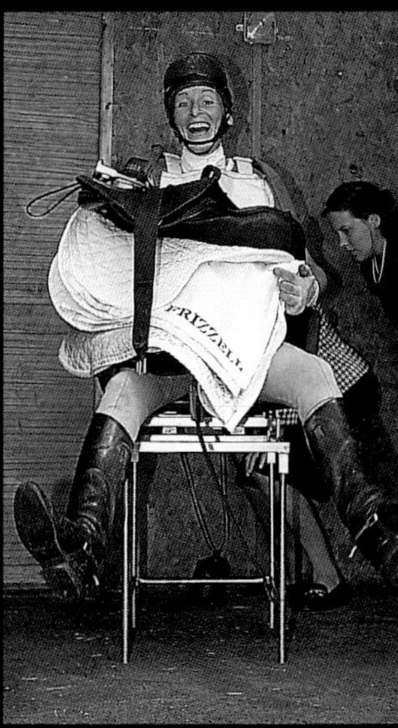

13

14

15

FIRST AID Competition horses are bound to incur a variety of knocks, cuts and scratches as a result of the sort of work they have to do; even at home, fitness work requires long hacks when they might just shy at something and, whilst unbalanced, knock into themselves. While cross-country schooling or competing, a common injury is for the horse to over-reach – when the hind foot strikes into the heel of the front foot – or he might suffer scratches or bruising if he doesn't clear a fence properly; and obviously more serious injuries can occur if he actually falls. So part of Annie's job is to be well versed in administering first aid.

'Any small cuts or grazes are treated by first trimming away the hair around the wound, and then cleaning it well with a surgical scrub. If it is anything more than just a slight graze then I bandage on a warm Animalintex poultice. This helps to continue to clean the wound and will draw out any infection that might be inside. If, when I take the poultice off the next day it looks as if there might be more pus or dirt to come out, a fresh poultice is applied. If, however, it all looks clean and healthy, it is given another wash with surgical scrub and is then sprayed with antiseptic wound spray or powder. After that, Dermobion cream is applied to the wound each day until the cut has healed over completely; this cream helps to prevent proud flesh forming and speeds up the healing process.

'We have a well stocked medicine cupboard in the yard, and a smaller, simpler first-aid kit in the lorry. At the events where we compete there is nearly always a vet present, and he would have the necessary equipment to deal with any major injuries that might occur; otherwise we take all we need to deal with those minor problems that we feel happy to handle ourselves. The lorry first-aid kit would contain cotton wool, rolls of gamgee, salt, surgical scrub, Dermobion cream and purple antiseptic spray, vetwraps, (stretchy, self-adhesive bandages), stable bandages, Savlon, scissors, various surgical dressings, Animalintex, syringes (for syringing bute in water down a horse's throat should we need to administer a painkiller or anti-inflammatory, or to introduce surgical scrub into a deeper wound to help clean it) and finally a thermometer. Also, Mary is quite often given various new products to try out, so the kit often contains extra goodies as well!'

PREVENTATIVE TREATMENTS 'Preventing a problem or injury is always preferable to having to treat something that could have been avoided. The most generally accepted practice is to poultice and bandage a horse's legs after a cross-country round, and/or to apply cold leg treatment if there is any concern about the well-being of the tendons. So whenever any of our horses run across country their legs are always treated afterwards with a clay poultice such as IceTight; this helps to compromise any concussion or bruising the horse may have suffered, and to bring down any slight swellings that might have occurred. Having washed the horse down we would first check his legs for cuts or scratches – IceTight should not be applied to broken skin, so these are cleaned and dressed with a small piece of Animalintex poultice. The IceTight is applied all round the legs, paying particular attention to the tendon area and the fetlock joints. Damp brown paper is wrapped round the legs to stop the poultice sticking to everything, and damp gamgee bandaged in place with stable bandages. These are left on overnight and the legs hosed off in the morning and again checked for heat or swelling.

'If there are any signs of swelling in the tendon area after the horse has finished his work, whether at home or at a competition, then it is essential to apply cold therapy on the suspected injury site immediately. With a horse like Conker, whom we knew had a tendon problem which might have well recurred at any time, cold therapy is used as a matter of course after any fastwork; in this case bags of crushed ice are bandaged to his legs. Ice will very readily cause blistering so it should never be held directly against the skin; I always play extra safe and wrap the bags of ice in damp tea towels and then bandage these in place. Even with this precaution I would only leave ice on the legs for ten minutes at a time, repeating the application every ten minutes for two or three more times before IceTighting and bandaging as normal.

'At home his legs would be hosed with cold water for fifteen minutes even after just normal exercise as well.

'There are several different cold therapy boots and gadgets that you can buy, such as gel pads that can be frozen and bandaged on instead of ice; or hosing boots, like big wellington boots which the horse stands in while water is circulated around inside them.'

THE ROAD TO RECOVERY 'Any injury to the limbs which involves box-rest for more than just a few days subsequently requires a careful programme of rebuilding the horse's fitness and strength. For example both Apple, who cracked a bone in his leg, and Conker who strained his tendon, had to start their fitness programme with controlled exercise: this means leading them out at walk without a rider, so their legs are carrying the least possible weight, and carefully controlling what they are allowed to do. The horse should always be led out in a bridle so that you have maximum control over him, because he could do untold damage to himself if he got away from you, or if you were having to haul him round in circles to stop him pulling away from you.

'The exercise period usually starts as a ten-minute session on relatively flat going, and after a few days the horse would be led out twice during the day for a ten-minute walk. After a week this would be built up to fifteen minutes twice a day. If everything was looking good, then in the third week he would be ridden out at walk for, say, twenty minutes to half an hour to begin with. During all this time he is kept stabled – having taken so much care about controlling how much exercise he is allowed, there is no point in then turning him out in a field where he can gallop around as much as he wishes and undo all your good work. During the week that he is being ridden, the exercise period would gradually be increased to, say, forty-five minutes and then to an hour. We would start to include some of our hillier rides at this point.

'After a month of walking, trotwork would be introduced, perhaps for only five minutes a day over the first few days, then gradually building up to what he would do in normal roadwork exercise. After two weeks of trotting, canterwork is started again. During all this time great care should be taken regarding the type of surface the horse is allowed to work on, and hard and bumpy ground should be avoided. Thus it may be necessary to travel to an all-weather gallop for his first canterwork, to be sure that everything is as safe and comfortable for him as possible. After Boris had recovered from his suspensory ligament injury and we were trying to build his fitness back up, the ground became far too hard to continue his canterwork so we took him swimming a few times so that his fitness could continue to improve without risking a recurrence of the injury.

'Once the horse is trotting and cantering in his everyday roadwork, then Mary might start some quiet, undemanding schooling to supple and fitten him; at this stage he would also be considered fit enough to turn out again. And if the patient in question was of an excitable temperament, as King Kong, he would be doped before he was turned loose so that he was less likely to celebrate his new-found freedom by galloping about madly.

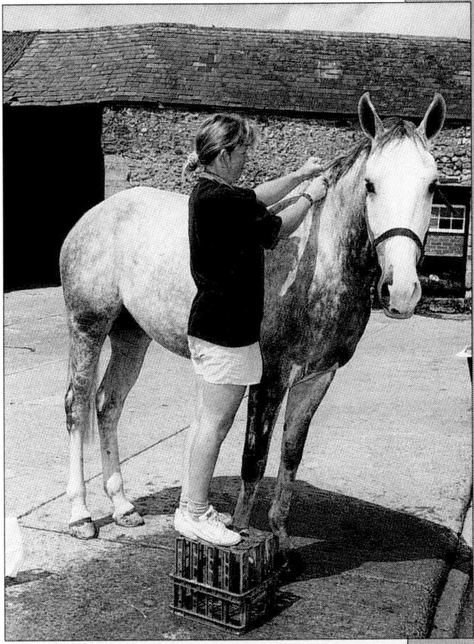

'Once the horse had been in work for at least eight weeks, his work programme would be the same as it was before his injury.'

COPING WITH DISASTERS 'When a horse is seriously injured, it is most important not to panic, but to think logically about what to do for the best. He is your responsibility, and panic and tears are not going to help him; he needs you to keep calm. Obviously any accident is very upsetting but it is important to put *his* needs first. At an event there are plenty of people around to help, but the main priority is first to make the accident site safe so there is no risk of any further casualties or injuries. So for example on the cross-country course the officials will stop the competition until the horse is moved clear of the course.

'As far as injuries are concerned, the first necessity is to stop excessive bleeding and to immobilise any limb which you may suspect is badly injured. Bleeding is stopped by applying a pressure bandage or tourniquet, and a suspected broken limb is immobilised using big rolls of gamgee and crêpe bandages, bound securely up and down the leg so that the joints are all kept straight and still. At a competition, probably you would not have to administer this emergency first aid yourself as there will almost certainly be a vet to hand; but if something happens at home in the yard, then those are the priorities. If you are on your own you must first make sure the horse is in a safe place, or make it safe if you can't move him; then arrest any serious bleeding and if necessary immobilise any traumatised limb, before rushing to contact the vet.

'Any injury or fall is upsetting, and as the groom you will be equally concerned for both horse and rider, however, there are usually plenty of people to care for the rider, and it is your responsibility to know how to help the horse. And then once the incident has been dealt with, you have to put it behind you – other than making sure you learn any particular lesson from it – and look ahead. If you let yourself worry about it happening again, or torment yourself about how much worse it could have been, you will never be in a fit state to do your job. What I do know is that all the horses in Mary's yard receive the best possible care: she never takes any short-cuts regarding their well-being, and perhaps most importantly, she prepares and trains them properly for the task ahead, and then rides them carefully and responsibly. And that is the best insurance you can have against injuries or accidents. So no matter what happens, I always know that everything possible has been, and will be done to help the horse.'

FEEDING The feeding of a competition horse plays a vital part in his fitness and competition programme. Too much or too little energy in the diet can result in disappointing performances, and as a general rule too much food leads to an overweight horse which is harder to get fit and more prone to leg injuries and strains. Mary takes charge of feeding all the horses in the yard, often making small changes to their diet depending on how they feel as she is working and competing them. She explains:

'Generally I try to make sure the novice horses are turned out as much as possible, often leaving them out all night and keeping them in during the day. It is far more natural for a horse to be out as much as possible, and the fitness required to compete at novice level can still be achieved without stabling them for too much of the time. I prefer to underestimate a horse's energy requirement until it has been out to an event or two – there is nothing more annoying than it becoming overexcited at an event simply because it has been overfed. I use the Spillers range of horse feeds and select different types of feed according to the energy input each particular horse needs, and whether or not that horse needs to gain or lose weight.

'The novice horses usually have a mixture of Cool Mix and Horse and Pony Nuts, bulked out with some chaff. I add a teaspoon of salt to the evening feed once they start their fastwork, to help replace any salts lost through sweating. If I feel they need more energy in their diet than this provides, then they might have some HDF cubes – High Digestible Fibre Cubes, or maybe Racecourse Cubes, along with chaff and salt. The quantities I feed vary between about 6lb and 12lb [2.7 and 5.4kg] of hard feed per day. Usually I give only two haynets each day, one in the morning and one at night, but any horse that needs to put on condition would get a third haynet at lunchtime. My general principle is, the fatter the horse, the thinner the haynet! I have haynets in three different sizes, holding 3½lb, 5lb or 7lb [1.6, 2.3 or 3.2kg] of of forage. The hard feed is given three times a day.

'The ratio between the amount of hard feed and forage alters depending on the sort of work the horse is doing: as a rough guide, novices would probably start on 70 per cent forage to 30 per cent concentrate feed, gradually changing to a 50:50 ration once they are competing. The more advanced horses would gradually receive more hard feed and less forage, until they are on 30 per cent forage to 70 per cent concentrate feed. I would never feed less than 25 per cent forage in the diet as the horse's gut stops functioning properly if the forage intake is too low, and disposes him to colic.

'All the horses are turned out day and night at the end of the eventing season. Throughout November there is usually sufficient grass for them to live on, but as it gets colder then they start to have hard feed and hay in the field. As they are getting plenty of fibre from the grass and hay, the hard feed I give them is quite high in energy, as they need extra energy in order to keep warm. They might have a mixture of Competition Nuts or Stud Cubes, fed once a day. So they may well have a higher energy diet while they are out in the field than they do when they actually come back in and start work.'

INVALIDS AND RECUPERATERS 'If a horse is off work, either through injury or illness, and particularly if he is to be box-rested, then his hard food is cut right back; otherwise he will be receiving an excess of energy – giving feed and nutrients which he cannot utilise because he is confined in his stable. Overfeeding would result in him putting on too much weight, his legs might become puffy and filled, and if his diet is too high in protein this can show as bumps under his skin – all in all he will not settle down into the quiet, calm routine that is needed to help him recover. So he might have just a little feed of something like Cool Mix, its purpose being more to give him something else to think about, rather than for any good it may do him – although having said that, it is vital to continue to give a concentrate feed if the horse has to receive in-feed medication; Apple, Diver's Rock and Conker for example would all have had bute in their feed to help reduce any pain and swelling. Diver's Rock also had to have Warfarin in his food as part of his treatment for navicular. A recuperating horse would have virtually ad-lib hay as long as he did not start to put on too much weight.

'We do like to organise things so as to keep the horse interested in life and still feeling part of the team. So if we are working in the yard we might let the patient out of his stable and either tie him up outside for a change of scene, or let him wander quietly round the yard loose. He would have his mane and tail washed every so often, and be kept groomed and trimmed so that he still felt loved and pampered!

'Both Apple and Diver's Rock proved to be excellent patients. Conker, however, took longer to settle to the idea, and would pace around his box messing up his bed and knocking over his water buckets; but as he lost his fitness he settled down.'

AFTERWORD

I HAVE LEARNED SO MUCH over the years of bringing on young horses and gradually producing them to the top level, but the learning curve is endless: every horse is so different. My two-and-a-half years working for Sheila Willcox, the ex-international three-day event rider, gave me a solid base for my stable management and riding experience. I owe a tremendous amount to Miss Willcox for the time and effort she put into teaching me; without it I'm sure I would never have made it to the top.

'Horses are such wonderful creatures to work with, and I feel that it is a real honour to have worked with characters such as Boris and William: Boris, with his generosity, unselfishness and honesty was such a fabulous horse to learn on, and William, the noble gentleman, whose good looks have won the hearts of thousands. He really put me "on the map", giving me my first four-star win, and first British team appearance. His endless string of top-level wins, interspersed with our infamous showjumping disasters, have definitely been character-building for me – and for everyone else involved with us! Anyway, his continuous victories would probably have become boring had it not been for the erratic showjumping phase!

'Every event rider's career has its highs and lows, and mine is no exception. The most memorable success was winning the prestigious Badminton Horse Trials in 1992 – that was certainly a dream come true! Competing at two Olympic Games has been such an honour. but with such heartbreaking results. I have been lucky enough to have had a couple of marvellous runs of success, notably five three-day event wins in a row in 1991/2, and a fabulous run of four major event wins during the autumn of 1996, after the disappointment of the Atlanta Olympics. The good times have certainly made up for the bad!

'Marrying David, the original "King", and giving birth to Emily, has helped to make my life even more complete. She is such a bundle of joy, and seems to be in her element travelling to almost all the events with me, where she is looked after by my wonderful mother while I am competing. Despite the many warnings I received, Emily hasn't changed my competitive spirit at all; as well as being determined to be a good mother, I'm as keen as ever to strive for perfection with my horses, and have my sights set firmly on the Sydney Olympics in the year 2000.

'I will never be able to repay Gill Robinson for all her tremendous support and enthusiasm over the years. The horses' happiness is of the utmost importance to her, and I have never felt any owner pressure from her at all, which hopefully results in our "Kings" leading the fair life they all deserve. I am also permanently indebted to my parents and David, who provide me with the best ever backup team. My mother deserves her own gold medal for all she does for me.

'And then there is Annie...what can I say, except the biggest ever thank-you for wholeheartedly devoting such a large part of your life to me, and especially:

'To all the Kings' horses!'

Above: Henry, who was with Mary briefly in 1996, has *almost* the last word!
Page 128: Mary and Star Appeal on their way to their Burghley win in 1996

39
FENCE